How to Start
Cloud Computing

Jim Gatenby

BERNARD BABANI (publishing) LTD
The Grampians
Shepherds Bush Road
London W6 7NF
England

www.babanibooks.com

Please Note

Although every care has been taken with the production of this book to ensure that all information is correct at the time of writing and that any projects, designs, modifications and/or programs, etc., contained herewith, operate in a correct and safe manner and also that any components specified are normally available in Great Britain, the Publishers and Author do not accept responsibility in any way for the failure (including fault in design) of any project, design, modification or program to work correctly or to cause damage to any equipment that it may be connected to or used in conjunction with, or in respect of any other damage or injury that may be so caused, nor do the Publishers accept responsibility in any way for the failure to obtain specified components.

Notice is also given that if equipment that is still under warranty is modified in any way or used or connected with home-built equipment then that warranty may be void.

© 2019 BERNARD BABANI (publishing) LTD

First Published – November 2019

British Library Cataloguing in Publication Data:

A catalogue record for this book is available from the British Library

ISBN 978-0-85934-779-2

Printed and bound in Great Britain for Bernard Babani (publishing) Ltd

About this Book

The Cloud is a metaphor for the storage of software and data on remote *Web server computers* around the world, managed by giant companies such as Microsoft and Google. If you've used services such as e-mail, *online* banking and shopping and social networking you have already been using Cloud Computing.

Other important tasks such as Self-Assessment Income Tax Returns, filing small business accounts and checking car records can now be done in the Cloud, i.e. online to the Internet.

Cloud Computing can provide huge savings in time and money for businesses, schools, colleges, etc. Recent years have seen these benefits spread to *individual users*. Instead of a bulky desktop computer, many important tasks can now be done in the Cloud, using a cheap, slimline computer running *web-based programs* or *apps* in a Web browser such as Chrome, Edge or Firefox, etc. These lightweight computers include tablets, smartphones and Chromebook and Cloudbook laptops. There's no need to buy and install expensive software — it's all provided and managed by professional staff in the Cloud *data centres*.

It's worth understanding Cloud Computing thoroughly, to cope with important chores such as Tax Returns, etc. Also to manage personal computing tasks such as *sharing* your documents and photos online, including sending an *e-mail link* to friends and colleagues, with options for them to *view* and *edit* documents.

Backing up your files and photos to the Cloud and accessing them on *any computer, anywhere* is discussed. This is cheaper and more efficient than stand-alone operation and compensates for the limited storage on mobile devices. Other features such as free Cloud file storage and subscription plans for extra storage are also discussed.

This book uses simple, non-technical language and clear, step-by-step instructions with screenshots.

No previous computing knowledge is assumed.

About the Author

Jim Gatenby trained as a Chartered Mechanical Engineer and initially worked at Rolls-Royce Ltd using computers in the analysis of jet engine performance. He obtained a Master of Philosophy degree in Mathematical Education by research at Loughborough University of Technology and taught mathematics and computing in school before becoming a full-time author. His most recent teaching posts included Head of Computer Studies and Information Technology Coordinator. The author has written over forty books in the fields of educational computing and Microsoft Windows, as well as several titles for Android tablets and smartphones.

Trademarks

Android, Google, Google Drive, Google Chrome, Chromebook, Chrome OS, Google Docs, Sheets, and Slides and Google Cloud Print are trademarks or registered trademarks of Google, Inc. Microsoft Windows, Office, Office 365, OneDrive, Word, Excel, PowerPoint, Edge and Internet Explorer are trademarks or registered trademarks of Microsoft Corporation. Dropbox is a trademark of Dropbox, Inc. Firefox is a trademark of Mozilla Foundation. iOS, iPhone, iPad, macOS, Mac and Safari are trademarks of Apple, Inc. LibreOffice is a trademark of the Document Foundation.

All other brand and product names used in this book are recognized as trademarks or registered trademarks of their respective companies.

Acknowledgements

I would like to thank my wife Jill for her support during the preparation of this book and also Michael Babani for making the project possible.

Contents

What is a Computer?

Introduction

This book is based on the use of computers in the *Cloud*. This term can be very confusing, especially if you're new to computing. So this chapter is intended to explain the basic features common to all types of computer including desktops, laptops, tablets and smartphones and also the mainframe computers used in large organisations. This should make it easier to understand the Cloud and why it is seen by many people as the future of computing.

If you're already familiar with the basic features of computers you may wish to skip straight to Chapter 2.

The Main Stages in Computing

All types of computer such as desktops, laptops, tablets, smartphones and the mainframe computers used in large organisations all have the following 4 stages:

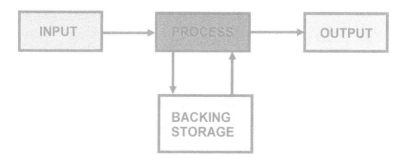

The above stages are discussed on the next few pages.

The Input Stage

This may involve the entry of raw *data* into the computer, such as numbers, names and addresses, photos, music and sound. Data is usually input using a keyboard. Data and *software* (i.e. *programs*) may also be copied from other computers. Other input devices such as *mice* and *touchpads* are discussed later in this book.

The Process Stage

Programs or Apps

After data is input into a computer, it is operated on by a computer *program*. The program is a set of instructions written in a special computer language based on English words. While the instructions are being carried out the program is said to be *running* or being *executed*. As an example of what a piece of programming or *code* looks like, a very short program in the popular Python programming language is shown below.

```
1   counter = 1
2   while counter < 11:
3       display.scroll ("Hi, Everyone")
4       counter=counter + 1
5       sleep(5000)
```

The result is to display a message on the screen ten times.

Programs are available for many different *applications*, or *apps* for short. Apps might be for word processing, drawing, editing a photo, accounts, games, booking a holiday, etc.

Programs are generally known as *software*, to distinguish them from the physical components of a computer such as the keyboard, screen and micro chips, known as *hardware*.

The Central Processing Unit (CPU)

This is often said to be the "brains" of any computer. The CPU carries out the instructions or *statements* in a program, such as line 3 on the previous page, which scrolls the message "Hi, Everyone" across the screen.

The speed of the CPU to execute instructions, known as the *clock speed*, is critical to the performance of a computer. Devices with fast processors are more expensive.

The Random Access Memory (RAM)

The RAM is *temporary* storage inside the computer. This holds the instructions and data for the program currently being run or executed. The instructions and data have to be transferred from the RAM to the CPU in what is known as the *fetch-execute* cycle. Programs and data in the RAM are lost when the computer is switched off.

The size of the RAM, like the speed of the CPU, is critical to the performance of any computer. It's a relatively easy task to add extra RAM, in the form of plug-in *memory chips*, to a large desktop or PC computer tower. It's also possible, but less straightforward, to increase the RAM on some laptops, tablets and smartphones.

An understanding of the functions of components such as the *RAM* and *CPU* above and the *backing storage* discussed on the next page is essential to appreciate the advantages of Cloud computing, on which this book is based.

The Output Stage

This often takes the form of text, numbers, photos, images, computer graphics and designs displayed on a screen or printed on paper. Output may also include sounds, music, speech and signals to control machines used in manufacturing or in surgical operations, for example. Other applications of computer robotics include remote controlled tractors, lawn mowers, self-drive cars and robots used in dangerous applications such as bomb disposal.

Backing Storage

Internal Storage

As mentioned earlier, programs and data are temporarily stored in the RAM while being used, but they are lost when the computer is switched off. So that programs and data can be used in future without being input again, they are permanently saved on *Backing Storage*, also known as *Internal Storage*. In the past this has usually been a *hard drive* inside the computer and consisting of several magnetic discs rotating at high speeds.

Many computers now use *SSDs* (*Solid State Drives*) for Internal Storage. An SSD uses *flash memory*, having no moving parts. These are faster and lighter than hard drives.

Files

Programs and data saved on a hard drive or SSD can be retrieved and loaded into the RAM when needed. They can also be deleted from the hard drive or SSD and replaced with new versions. A program or block of data is saved on backup storage as a *file*, with a meaningful *filename*.

A *data file* contains text and numbers which may be processed and converted into meaningful information.

A *program file* contains statements or instructions which can be *executed* i.e. carried out by a computer.

The filename is listed in a *file manager* program so that it can found and retrieved easily. Files can be edited, renamed and resaved when necessary. Files can also be organised within named *folders* holding groups of related files.

External Storage

This refers to *removable* devices like *external hard drives* and *SSDs*, *SD cards*, *flash drives/memory sticks*, discussed later. These are usually plugged into a *port*, i.e. a connecting socket on the computer. Older devices used *magnetic tape* drives for backing storage like those used in tape recorders for music.

Binary Code

A computer is a *two-state device*, like a switch or a light bulb, which is either On or Off. So it cannot directly represent the digits 0 to 9 or the letters of the alphabet.

All numbers and letters, etc., entered into a computer are translated or *coded* into patterns based only on the numbers 0 and 1, known as *binary digits* or *bits* for short. The computer uses *transistors*, i.e. very small switches, which are On or Off and can therefore represent 0 and 1.

A *byte* is a group of 8 bits and is used to represent the digits 0-9, the upper and lower case letters of the alphabet and other keyboard characters. A byte can also represent an *instruction*. Some examples are shown on the next page from the *ASCII* code, (*American Standard Code for Information Interchange*). Only 7 bits are actually used as the code, with the eighth bit used for checking purposes.

Some examples of keyboard characters in the 7-bit ASCII binary code are shown below:

Character	Code
A	1 0 0 0 0 0 1
B	1 0 0 0 0 1 0
d	1 1 0 0 1 0 0
e	1 1 0 0 1 0 1
3	0 1 1 0 0 1 1
4	0 1 1 0 1 0 0
+	0 1 0 1 0 1 1
=	0 1 1 1 1 0 1

Binary codes are also used to represent *instructions* and the *addresses* or *store locations* of data in the RAM. As shown below, the *HEX* or *Hexadecimal code* uses letters of the alphabet and the digits 0-9 as a form of shorthand to represent *4 bits* or a *nibble*. This example is an instruction to load data into the CPU.

	Instruction		Address of data in memory			
Binary	1010	1101	1011	1111	1100	0111
Hex	A	D	B	F	C	7

Programs written in a programming language such as Python or JavaScript, using English words, are translated into *machine code* (binary or hexadecimal) for use in the CPU. This is done by an *interpreter* or a *compiler* program.

Units of Data Storage

As mentioned on the previous two pages, data such as letters are translated into a 7-bit binary code with an eighth bit used for checking, known as the *parity* bit. The byte or group of 8-bits is the basic unit for stating the capacity of a computer's memory, as shown below.

1 Kilobyte (KB) = 1024 Bytes

1 Megabyte (MB) = 1024 Kilobytes

1 Gigabyte (GB) = 1024 Megabytes

1 Terabyte (TB) = 1024 Gigabytes

1 Petabyte (PB) = 1024 TB

Some very approximate examples of the amount of memory or storage space are shown below:

A page of plain text	10-20KB
This chapter in this book	160KB
A photograph	1-3MB
A 10 minute video	1GB

- Hard drives and SSDs typically have storage capacities of 128GB-500GB, with 1TB-6TB also available.

- Common RAM capacities are 2GB, 4GB and 8GB.

- As discussed in detail later in this book, increasing use of the Cloud will mean such high storage capacities are not needed on our personal computers.

The Internet and World Wide Web

The *Internet* is a global *network of networks*, connecting millions of super computers by fibre optic-cables, copper wires, TV cables, satellites and Wi-Fi, etc. The *World Wide Web* is millions of *Web pages* of information on *Web servers* all over the world.

Web Browser

This is an app such as Google Chrome, Firefox, Safari and Internet Explorer, used to view Web pages after a *search* using a *search engine* such as Google.

Cloud Computing

This is the use of Internet *Web servers*, discussed above, to store data and run our programs from our own computers, known as *Web clients*, accessed by a Web browser like Google Chrome. Microsoft and Google, for example, have millions of servers in large Cloud *data centres* in huge buildings in many different countries. As discussed in Chapter 3, there are many advantages in using the Clouds and the *Client/ Server* model.

User Interface

This is the way we interact with a computer using hardware such as the keyboard, touchpad or mouse and the various screen displays or *desktop*s containing *icons* and *menus*.

Icons are small images on the screen which can be selected or clicked to launch an application such as a word processor. A menu displays a list of clickable options.

The interface also includes software such as a Web browser. This allows us to send requests to the Internet, execute programs and display the output on the screen.

2

The Evolution of the Personal Computer

Introduction

My first experience of using computers was in the Performance Office at Rolls-Royce in the late 1960s. In those days we used *mainframe* computers to process numerical data collected during the testing of jet engines.

The programs and data were written on paper by hand and copied onto *punched cards* using a machine like a large typewriter, with fixed positions containing either a hole or no hole. A hole represented 1 and no hole represented 0. This enabled binary codes for numbers, letters and other keyboard characters, as discussed on page 6, to be represented in 80 positions along the card.

The cards were collected from various R-R departments and taken by trolley to the mainframe computer in another building. A *card reader* scanned the cards by shining light through the holes, producing electronic pulses input as bytes into the *RAM*. These bytes represented the programs and data to be executed in the *CPU*, discussed in Chapter 1.

Output from the mainframe computer was printed on paper and returned to the relevant department together with the deck of cards. (Continuous *punched tapes* were also used instead of punched cards in some applications.)

The use of punched cards on a mainframe computer was laborious by today's standards. However, using a remote computer to process your data is similar in principle to Cloud Computing on which this book is based.

Early Personal Computers

Having moved into maths teaching in the seventies, my first involvement with personal computers (or *microcomputers* as they were then known) was around 1978, when the school acquired two Commodore Pet machines. The Pet was a heavy desktop machine with keyboard, screen, CPU, RAM, etc., all housed in a single metal case.

Many other personal computers arrived in the seventies and early eighties, such as the Commodore 64, VIC 20, BBC Micro, Sinclair Spectrum and ZX 81 and the Apple 1.

The BBC Micro

The BBC Micro, developed by Acorn Computers, was selected to be used in the BBC Computer Literacy Project. This also included a television series called The Computer Programme. The BBC Micro sold over 1.5 million machines and was used in many British schools, along with its rival, the Research Machines RML 380Z.

A feature of the BBC Micro was that software such as the Wordwise word processor and the ViewSheet spreadsheet could be bought on a *ROM* (*Read Only Memory*) chip and plugged inside the computer. These programs were much faster to load into RAM than those stored on *cassette tape* or the *magnetic floppy disk*, discussed on the next page.

The ARM Processor

Acorn went on to develop further machines including the Acorn Electron for home users and the powerful Acorn Archimedes RISC Machine. *RISC (Reduced Instruction Set Computer)* means the processor uses fewer instructions, enabling it to operate much faster. ARM processors are now dominant, in 2019, in the latest smartphones and tablets.

Storage

Cassette tapes were a slow form of backing storage, since to find a particular program or piece of data you had to read sequentially through the tape. *Magnetic floppy disks* soon replaced cassette tapes as they could access stored programs and data more quickly. Disks were inserted into a *floppy disk drive* and accessed by a movable *read/write head*.

Hard disk drives were introduced in the eighties. These contain several built-in magnetic discs revolving at high speed on a central spindle.

An Internal Hard Disk Drive

The first hard drive I used had a storage capacity of 20MB compared with many of today's drives typically having 500GB or 1TB. Although initially separate plug-in devices, hard drives were later built into computers as standard. These are known as the *Internal Storage* and contain the installed programs or apps and the data such as names, addresses, documents, games or photos and other images. The hard drive also contains the *operating system*, i.e. the software used to control the running of the computer, regardless of what program or app is being executed.

Hard drives, both internal and external, are still widely used today, although being replaced in some computers by the *SSD* (*Solid State Drive*). This is a form of *flash memory*, which has no moving parts and operates faster than the hard drive.

The IBM PC launched in 1981 was the start of a series of desktop computers which still dominate in business and other large organisations today. *IBM compatible* computers were developed which used the same *MSDOS Microsoft Disk Operating System* software to control the basic functions of the computer. These came from many other manufacturers such as Compaq, Dell and Hewlett-Packard. IBM compatible computers, or simply PCs, have dominated the desktop computer market for many years, the only other popular brand being the Apple range, such as the Mac.

An IBM Compatible Desktop Computer

Expandability

The IBM compatible PC desktop machines were generally large and easy to take apart and reassemble. You didn't need to be a skilled computer technician. In fact it was quite a simple job to buy a kit of parts and assemble your own PC from scratch. Similarly you could easily improve the performance of an existing computer by:

1. Installing a bigger hard drive as shown on page 11, to increase your Internal Storage.

2. Plugging in some extra memory (RAM) chips, as shown below.

RAM (Random Access Memory) Chips

3. Inserting a faster processor into the CPU socket on the computer's *motherboard*, i.e. the large circuit board containing many of the microchips, *databuses* and other electronic components inside the computer.

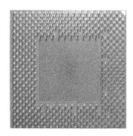 

CPU/Microprocessor   CPU Socket on Motherboard

Early Programming

In the early days programs weren't available to buy on disc or tape or download from the Internet as you can now. You had to write your own programs on paper, type them in at the keyboard and save them on a cassette tape.

Most programming used the *BASIC* language *(Beginners All-purpose Symbolic Instruction Code)*. As well as teaching programming to school students, evening classes were started to teach programming to adults of all ages.

Early programs consisted of numbered statements as shown in the small example on page 2. These all had to be entered into the computer's memory before the program could be *run* or *executed*.

Operating System Commands

These are single words typed in at the keyboard without the line numbers used in program statements. Commands are still used today for some tasks. When the **Return** key is pressed the command is carried out immediately. A few examples from *MSDOS (Microsoft Disk Operating System)*, as used on PC machines, are given below.

cls	clear the screen
copy	copy a file
del	delete a file
defrag	defragment or reorganise a hard drive
format	erase a hard drive and prepare for use

Some keywords such as **PRINT** in Basic can be used both as operating system commands to be executed immediately or as numbered statements executed as part of a program.

The GUI (Graphical User Interface)

Many people didn't have the time or the skills to write long programs or remember lots of operating system commands to be typed in at the keyboard. One small spelling mistake or missed punctuation mark can cause a program to fail.

In the early 1980s, instead of text-based systems just described, Xerox and Apple developed the *Graphical User Interface*, a system of controlling a computer by "*pointing and clicking*" objects on the screen using a *mouse* to move a *cursor*, also known as a *pointer*.

Select

3-Button Mouse

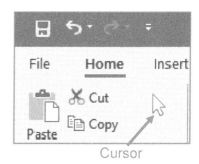

Cursor

The screen objects include *icons*, as shown below on the *desktop*, the main screen for launching programs or apps. Icons usually represent programs or websites, discussed shortly. Simply click or double-click the left mouse button with the cursor over an icon to start running a program.

Icons on the Desktop

The GUI also includes lists of options or *menus* which pop up on the screen after you select headings such as **File** or **Home** shown below. The example below shows the **File** menu in the Microsoft Word word processing program, with options to **Save** and **Print** a document, etc.

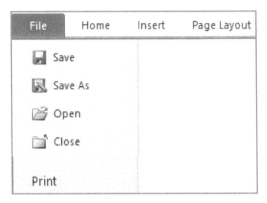

The *right button* on a mouse, shown on page 15, can be clicked to display a menu relevant to the current position of the cursor or pointer.

The Apple Macintosh was the first to use this new way to operate a computer, also known as a *WIMP* system (Windows, Icons, Mouse and Pointer). Information is entered and displayed on the screen in rectangular boxes known as *windows*.

In 1985 Microsoft developed its own graphical user interface, known as *Microsoft Windows*. The IBM PC and the many other brands of IBM compatible computers that use the Windows operating system now dominate the world of personal computers in business and education. These are generally referred to as PCs or Windows PCs. The Apple Mac is a popular alternative to the Windows PC but with a smaller share of the personal computer market.

The Need for More Processing Power

Since the launch of the first PCs in the eighties, demand for processing power has increased greatly. Computer programs or apps are now very sophisticated, with software such as Microsoft Word and the Excel spreadsheet being widely used in businesses, educational institutions and other large organisations all over the world. These programs are packed with many functions and user-friendly features making them easier to use, but requiring powerful computers to run them.

Multi-tasking

This is a feature of operating systems, such as Microsoft Windows and Apple Mac OS, and means the running of more than one program at the same time in one computer. This requires a fast, powerful processor and high capacity RAM or memory, as discussed in Chapter 1.

Multi-media

Computers are now much more versatile than in the early days. Data input and output doesn't just consist of plain text and numbers. Instead many people watch movies, listen to music, play video games and build up libraries of thousands of photos. All of these activities call for computers with more processing power, i.e. faster CPUs, bigger RAM, and greater Internal Storage, i.e. hard drive or SSD capacity, as discussed in Chapter 1.

As discussed in Chapter 3 and later, Cloud Computing can provide us with vastly increased storage capacity and more powerful processing, all accessible from a relatively modest desktop, laptop, tablet or smartphone computer using a Web browser program.

Mobile Computers

The desktop PC, as shown on page 12, has remained dominant in offices and other situations where it is required for regular use as part of the furniture. The need to use computers on the move led to the development of the *laptop* and its smaller relative the *notebook*, which both share the folding "clamshell" design shown immediately below.

Dell Laptop

Recent years have seen the introduction and massive sales of handheld *tablets* and *smartphones*, shown below.

9 inch Tablet   5 inch Smartphone

The laptop computer, as shown near the top of the previous page, is very similar to a desktop machine, apart from its compact layout. It is powered by a battery rather than the mains power unit used by the desktop machine. A *touchpad* is built into the keyboard to operate a laptop but a mouse can be used if preferred.

The tablet and smartphone were a very radical step forward. Despite their tiny size, they are still real computers with the essential stages of INPUT, PROCESS, OUTPUT and BACKING STORAGE as discussed in Chapter 1. Obviously because of their size they can't have a large hard drive as shown on page 11. However, as shown in the following table, the tablet and smartphone have good CPU speeds and RAM and vastly improved performance compared with early computers such as the BBC Micro.

Computer	CPU Speed	RAM	Storage
1981			
BBC Micro	2MHz	16/32KB	Cassette
2019			
Windows PC	2.5/4GHz	4/8GB	500GB/1TB
Apple Mac	4GHz	8GB	128/256GB
9 inch Tablet	2.3GHz	2GB	32/128GB
5 inch Smartphone	2.3GHz	2/4GB	16/64GB

Please see page 7 for definitions of KB, GB and TB.

GHz or GigaHertz is a measure of the speed of the CPU to carry out instructions. Currently 4GHz is a fast CPU speed.

Comparing Computers

As can be seen from the table on page 19, although the BBC Micro was at the forefront of technology in 1981, its performance has been eclipsed by modern devices.

When the first hard drives arrived for the BBC Micro their storage capacity was a very modest 20MB, a fraction of the storage of modern devices shown in the table on page 19. Similarly a CPU speed of 4GHz is over 2000 times faster than a speed of 2MHz. Also 2GB of RAM common today is equal to about 2000MB or about 2 million KB, compared with the meagre 16/32KB RAM in the BBC Micro.

CPU and RAM

The table also shows that the tiny iPad tablet and Android Smartphone have very good CPU speed and RAM, better than many full size computers and many times greater than the BBC Micro launched nearly 40 years ago.

Storage

Obviously tablets and smartphones can't be fitted with the bulky 500GB/1TB hard drives or SSDs used in desktop and laptop computers. It is possible to fit *external* hard drives and SSDs to smartphones and tablets to give extra storage. However this is not practical when using these handheld devices on the move. As discussed in the rest of this book, the Cloud provides large amounts of inexpensive, extra storage for all types of personal computer.

The Cloud enables you to access your data on *any computer*, *anywhere* in the world. This is particularly useful for mobile computers with their very limited Internal Storage.

The Internet and Cloud Computing

Introduction

The previous chapters discussed the development of personal computers, including their use to store data, information and images such as photos and videos.

Also to run or execute computer programs or apps, to carry out required tasks, such as typing a report or document in a word processor or producing a set of accounts or calculations in a spreadsheet program.

The increasing use of computers for work involving photos and videos has created a need for more computing power for executing programs and more capacity for the storage of data.

Initially personal computers were used as *standalone* devices.

- All data was stored onboard on hard disc drives, etc.
- Programs were executed in the CPU in the device.

The increased use of low storage capacity smartphones and tablets has also increased the need for extra storage facilities. This need can be met by the use of *Cloud Computing*, which may be defined as follows:

The use of powerful *remote* computers in *data centres* to provide *data storage* capacity and carry out *program execution* and *other services*, accessed over the Internet by the user of a *local client* or *personal computer* which can be a desktop, laptop, tablet or smartphone.

Local Area Networks

In the early 1970s, before the Internet became a household name, computers in schools, universities and businesses were connected together to share resources in a *LAN* or *Local Area Network*. The LAN might include perhaps 10 to 30 computers in a classroom or office, or perhaps up to a few hundred in a large business or organisation. The LAN enables every computer in a room, for example, to share a single printer. Instead of buying expensive copies of a software program such as a word processor, spreadsheet or learning package for each computer, a much more economical *network licence* could be bought.

The File Server

The *file server* is a central computer with high capacity hard disc drive for storing data files and programs or apps. Individual computers, known as *client*s are connected to the file server by cables or Wi-Fi. Early school networks used *Ethernet* cables and these are still in use today. This was an early example of the *client/server* model for requesting and receiving data and information from a powerful central computer. Early file servers were basically a file storage system, with the actual program execution being carried out on the client machines.

The Router

Modern computers, i.e. desktops, laptops, tablets and smartphones, now have built-in Wi-Fi, allowing them to connect wirelessly or with Ethernet cables to a central *hub* or *router* as shown on page 25. Then they can share a single printer, exchange files and connect to the Internet, as discussed later in this book.

Wide Area Networks

The LAN discussed on the previous page is used to allow multiple computers to share files, programs and a printer across a small network in a single room or office block, etc. However, many businesses and large organisations have LANs on different sites and these may need to communicate with each other. The Wide Area Network or WAN is a network of computers over a much larger area than the LAN on a single site. Each LAN is connected to the WAN using a *router* for communication with the computers on the other LANs and for the exchange of data.

The router uses a device called a *modem* either built in or standalone. This converts a computer's *digital data* (binary digits discussed on page 6) into the *sound waves* needed for transmission on a telephone network. Another router/modem at the receiving end converts the data back to the digital form required by the computer accepting the data.

The Internet

The first WANs were used for communication by voice and text messages. The Internet is a massive WAN and consists of millions of computers all over the world. Computers are mainly connected by cables using the telephone networks. In some areas, the cables laid for *cable television* are used for the Internet.

Some areas of the UK have the latest *fibre-optic cables* which allow data to be transmitted much faster than the standard copper cables still used in many areas.

Where there are no suitable network cables, such as on ships and aircraft or in remote rural areas, *satellites* can be used to transmit and receive data. However, these are relatively slow and can be affected by bad weather.

The Internet uses cables under the sea to communicate across the world. The first submarine cables were laid in the 19th century to carry text messages. Nowadays large companies such as Google are laying high speed fibre-optic cables to carry all sorts of data such as text, photos, sound, and video between computers all over the world.

Connecting to the Cloud

Cloud Computing, a metaphor for *services available on the Internet*, can be accessed from all sorts of computers — desktops, laptops, tablets and smartphones.

Broadband Wi-Fi

The general name for the transmission of data across the Internet is *broadband*. This replaced an earlier system known as *dial-up*. Broadband is much faster than dial-up and makes better use of the telephone cables, etc.

With dial-up you couldn't use the Internet and make a phone call at the same time. Broadband allows both to be used simultaneously.

Connecting Laptop and Desktop Computers

These normally have the necessary Wi-Fi adapters built in from new, allowing them to connect to the Internet via a home or office LAN. Otherwise the technology can be bought separately as a plug-in *dongle/memory stick* as shown below.

Wi-Fi Network Adapter Dongle

Internet Service Providers

To set up a home network, first open an account with an *ISP (Internet Service Provider)*, such as BT, Virgin Media, Sky or TalkTalk. Subscriptions of £20-£50 per month may include unlimited broadband data, phone calls and TV.

Broadband Router

Your ISP subscription should include a free *broadband router* or *hub*. The connecting ports for cables on a BT Home Hub are shown below.

BT Home Hub Network Router

The white port on the left above is used to connect the router via a short cable to a *splitter* or *microfilter*. The microfilter is connected to the *Broadband DSL (Digital Subscriber Line)* i.e. the broadband copper telephone cables. The microfilter has two ports to allow both the router and an ordinary telephone to share the same telephone cable.

Splitter or Microfilter

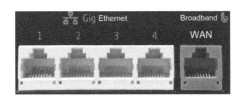

The four yellow ports shown above and at the bottom of the previous page allow computers on a home network to be connected by Ethernet cables rather than Wi-Fi.

The red port on the BT router labelled Broadband WAN can be used to connect your home network via an Ethernet cable to a Wide Area Network other than BT.

A label on the back of the router shown below gives the *Network Name* or *SSID (Service Set Identifier)* and the *Wireless Key* or *password* used to prevent unauthorised access to your network.

Smartphones

Smartphones also have built-in Wi-Fi, so you can use a smartphone to connect to a home Wi-Fi network and access the Cloud. The smartphone can also access the Cloud via a 3G/4G/5G *cell phone network* as discussed on page 28.

Computers with Wi-Fi capability can also connect to the Cloud when away from their home network using *public Wi-Fi hotspots* in cafes, hotels and on buses, etc.

Connecting to the Internet Using Wi-Fi

If you take out a subscription with an ISP, as discussed on page 25, a router and full instructions for connecting it to the Internet will be included. The general method of connecting to the Internet is similar for all types of computer equipped with Wi-Fi — Windows PCs and Android and Apple tablets and smartphones, as shown below.

From the **Settings** menu select Wi-Fi and make sure it is switched **On**. A list of networks within range of your router appears as partially shown on the left below. Select the name of your network This name or **SSID** should appear on the back of the router as shown on page 26. Then enter your router's wireless/password/key as shown on the right below and select CONNECT.

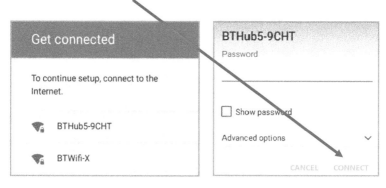

Once connected to the Internet you will be able to start using Cloud Computing and all the advantages it brings compared with working locally within the confines of your own computer — desktop, laptop, tablet or smartphone.

Cell Phone Networks

Smartphones communicate using radio waves with *towers* in areas around the country known as *cells*, enabling the transmitting and receiving of phone calls. The towers also allow smartphones and suitably equipped tablets and laptops to connect to the Internet using *3G/4G* technology for sending and receiving data such as documents and photos, etc. This means you can use the Internet and access the Cloud wherever you can get a signal for a mobile phone.

1G, 2G, 3G, 4G, 5G

These terms refer to the generations in the development of mobile phone communications technology. 4G is the latest standard on smartphones with 5G coming in the near future.

1G   Simple telephone calls only.

2G   Text messaging added to phone calls.

3G   Web browsing, email, video, photos.

4G   Like 3G but faster.

5G   The fastest so far, when available.

Some more expensive *tablets* have 3G/4G technology built in from new. You can also add 3G/4G technology to a tablet or a laptop using a *plug-in dongle* or *memory stick*. This will allow you to use a tablet or laptop on the move, where there is no Wi-Fi, using *mobile data*, just like a smartphone.

If you're using a smartphone or tablet, etc., with 3G/4G technology via an account with a cell phone network such as EE, Giffgaff, O2, Three, etc., follow the instructions provided to activate the SIM card and start using the Internet and hence the Cloud.

Essential Cloud Jargon

Data Centres

These are very large buildings containing many powerful computers. Large companies such as Google and Microsoft have data centres across America and worldwide.

Web Servers

These are computers in the data centres used to store data, host *websites* and execute *Web-based* apps or programs.

Clients

These are our own personal computers used to access the Web servers, which may be thousands of miles away.

World Wide Web or Web

Sir Tim Berners-Lee invented the World Wide Web. The Web is a collection of billions of *Web pages* stored in data centres around the world.

Web Page

This is a text document saved on a Web server which can also include images, videos and *links* to other Web pages.

Website

A group of related Web pages which have a unique name. Used as a source of information, to promote a business or to provide services such as online shopping, for example.

Web Browser

A program used to display Web pages and move between pages on a website. Also to access Web-based apps.

Search Engine

A program used to search the Web to find information, after entering *keywords* relevant to your chosen subject.

How Can We Use Cloud Computing?

Data centres mentioned on page 29 are the basis of the Cloud. The data centres (or "centers" in the USA) are operated by computing giants such as Google, Facebook and Microsoft. These each have numerous data centres, mainly in America but also in other parts of the world. Each data centre has thousands of Web server computers housed on racks on top of one another in vast buildings, so large that the staff use cycles to get around. Huge cooling systems are needed to dissipate the heat generated.

Data centres provide computing services for organisations such as Government agencies, educational institutions, banks and large businesses.

Individual Users of Data Centres

We can also access the data centres as individual users of personal client computers. We just need to connect our computer to the Internet via a Web browser and use the Cloud services. If you have used e-mail or instant messaging you've already used data centres in the Cloud.

Why Use the Cloud?

Recent years have seen an increase in the demand for more computing power on our own personal computers. Greater need for faster CPUs to cope with more sophisticated programs has coincided with a requirement for more storage for memory-hungry data such as photos and videos.

Personal computers with high performance CPUs and large capacity RAM and Internal Storage, (as discussed in Chapter 2), are very expensive.

Also tablets and smartphones are now widely used for many mainstream computing tasks but have very little Internal Storage for photos and documents, etc.

What Cloud Services are Available?

We can now use a Web browser on our computer to utilise the power of the Web servers in a remote data centre. The server can do all the heavy work, previously done entirely within the confines of our own computer. This is the client/server model as mentioned elsewhere in this book.

Some of the main Cloud-based activities available to the home user are:

- Using a Web browser to search for information on any subject, no matter how bizarre, such as flea treatment for cats

- Storing data such as photos, videos, and documents in Cloud services such as Microsoft OneDrive, Google Drive, Dropbox and iCloud Drive. Also sharing photos and videos with friends and relatives anywhere in the world.

- Executing Web-based programs on a Web server rather than on your computer. Web-based software includes Google Docs and Sheets and MS Office 365, which includes MS Word and MS Excel.

- Printing over the Internet to a designated printer anywhere in the world, using Google Cloud Print.

- Using services such as home banking, online shopping and Income Tax Returns.

- E-mail, messaging, video calls and social networking such as Facebook and Twitter.

- Netflix streaming of films and TV programs using AWS, (Amazon Web Services). AWS provides Cloud services for many large companies.

More Cloud Computing Jargon

Computing in general relies heavily on jargon and Cloud Computing is no exception. The acronyms *SaaS*, *PaaS* and *IaaS* are used by IT professionals to represent services available in the Cloud. They are roughly translated below.

SaaS: Software as a Service

The use of software, i.e. programs or apps installed, managed and executed on Web servers in the Cloud, accessed by a Web browser running on a client computer.

PaaS: Platform as a Service

This provides services in the Cloud to help software developers to create and test Websites and apps to be accessed or executed on the Web.

IaaS: Infrastructure as a Service

The storage of data on Web servers provided on systems such as Google Drive, OneDrive, Dropbox and iCloud Drive. Some storage is free, after which it's pay-as-you-go.

Where on Earth is the Cloud?

The Cloud is a good metaphor for the place where we store the data which we *upload* and *download* over the Internet — just like water vapour which evaporates from the earth and ascends to the real clouds in the sky, only to condense later and fall back to the earth as rain. The Cloud analogy is not strictly accurate since Internet data mainly travels in cables, which may be underground, on poles and under the sea. Cloud Computing is actually carried out *on earth in data centres* provided worldwide by the big computing companies. But the Cloud is still a helpful way to think of Internet services.

Advantages of Cloud Computing

The use of Cloud Computing is increasing because:

- You can access your data such as photos and documents, etc., using any Internet computer which you are signed into, anywhere in the world.

- Colleagues can work on the same document simultaneously and all can view the latest updated version of the document.

- The Cloud provides a secure backup service for your important photos and documents, etc.

- Web servers are managed by computing professionals and should be well maintained and housed in buildings with good security and restricted access.

- All the important software is stored on the servers and regularly *updated* by the staff in the data centre.

- The heavy workload of running programs is transferred from your computer to the Web servers in the Cloud. So you don't need a powerful client computer. Please see the notes on the Google Chromebook on page 35.

Security Issues

- Strong passwords are essential to prevent illegal access to your data.

- Internet cables under the sea have been damaged accidentally by ships anchors and fishermen. Also earthquakes, cyclones, tsunamis, shark bites.

- There is also a perceived threat of a hostile nation trying to cripple the Internet by cutting the undersea cables.

Google Drive

- Apart from its famous search engine, Google is one of the leading providers of Cloud Computing.

- *Google Drive* is a Cloud Storage system for saving your files, i.e. documents and photos, on Web servers.

- After signing up for a free *Google Account* you can access your files and photos on any Internet computer anywhere in the world.

- Google Drive provides *15GB of free storage* and you can pay a few pounds monthly to buy more.

- Google *Backup and Sync* automatically copies the latest versions of your files to the Drive Cloud folder.

- Google Drive includes the very popular free *Docs* wordprocessor, *Sheets* spreadsheet and *Slides* presentation software. Files are created *online* and can also be viewed and edited *offline* and have all the *essential* functions of Word and Excel, etc.

Docs   Sheets   Slides

- Files created in these apps don't count against your 15GB free storage in Google Drive.

- Google Drive can be used on all the main computer platforms and can import files saved in the universal Microsoft Office format.

- Files created in Google Drive can be *downloaded* and saved in formats compatible with Microsoft Office.

Google Drive and other Cloud Storage systems such as *OneDrive* and *Dropbox* are discussed later in this book.

Computers Designed for the Cloud

1. Google Chromebooks

This is a range of laptop computers intended for Cloud Computing and produced by leading companies such as Acer, Dell, HP, Asus and Samsung.

Acer Chromebook

The Chromebook is based on the leading Google Chrome browser. All the heavy work is done by the Web servers in the Cloud, so the Chromebook doesn't need such powerful and heavy internal components like other types of laptop.

As a result, the Chromebook has the following advantages:

- Very light and slim design.
- Inexpensive. Can be bought for under £150.
- Very fast and easy to start up and use.
- Built-in protection against malicious software .
- Excellent battery life: 10-12 hours between charges.
- Over 1 million apps available, many of them free.
- 100GB of free Google Drive Cloud Storage.

More information about the Chromebook is given in our companion title "An Introduction to Chromebook Computing" ISBN 978-0-859345934-777-8 from Bernard Babani (publishing) Ltd.

2. Cloudbooks: Windows 10 S Laptops

- *Windows 10 S* is a slimmed down version of Windows 10, which has over 800 million users. It is intended to compete with Chromebooks and their Chrome OS operating system.

- Microsoft Windows has its own *OneDrive* Cloud Storage system and can also use Google Drive, just discussed and *Dropbox*.

- OneDrive, Drive and Dropbox are discussed in more detail in later chapters of this book.

- Windows 10 S is pre-installed on relatively cheap, light and low specification PC laptops, known as Cloudbooks, made by coompanies such as HP, Acer, Asus, Samsung and Dell.

- For security, Windows 10 S can only use software downloaded from the Microsoft Store.

- Microsoft provides 5GB of OneDrive free Cloud Storage, with more available on subscription. (1TB is free for students)

- *Office 365* is Microsoft's *online software* including Word, Excel, PowerPoint and others, depending on your *monthly subscription plan* from £5.99 a month upwards. This also includes 1 TB of Cloud Storage. Office 365 is compatible with most computer platforms - Windows, Android, iOS, MacOS, etc.

4

Accessing the Cloud

Introduction

The *Cloud* is really billions of *Web pages* in *websites* stored on *Web server* computers in large *data centres* all over the world. This chapter looks in more detail at the following aspects of the Cloud:

- The various uses of Cloud websites.

- Important features of a website such as the *address* or *URL*, the *Web host* and the *domain name*.

- A brief overview of the creation of Web pages, including *HTML* and *hyperlinks* to other pages.

- *Uploading* or *publishing* Web pages to the Cloud.

- Displaying a website in a *Web browser*, after entering its *address* or *URL*.

- Using a *Search Engine* within a Web browser to find information from public websites, after entering relevant *keywords* in the *Search Bar*.

Words and terms highlighted in blue above are explained in detail in this chapter.

Chapter 5 discusses Web browsing in detail, including the use of *bookmarks* and *favourites* to list Web pages for future use. Later chapters cover the storing of your personal data and running Web-based programs in the Cloud instead of on the computer sitting on your desk or on your lap, etc.

Websites

A website is a group of Web pages on a particular subject. The purpose of the site might be to:

- Share the latest news, including photos, for your family, or for a community, village, school, etc.
- Advertise a business, including online sales.
- Share the latest information on a vast range of subjects, e.g. health, education, history, finance, etc. *Wikipedia* is a free, *online encyclopedia* displaying information on many subjects provided by volunteers worldwide.
- Publicise events such as sport, music and other entertainment and manage ticket sales.
- Display price comparisons from different suppliers of goods, utilities and other services.
- Show training videos and teach DIY.
- Social networking, such as Facebook, Twitter, etc.
- *Stream* films and TV programmes on Netflix.
- Show videos and play music, posted by members of the public on the *YouTube* website.
- Hold *online live auctions*, receiving bids from all over the world.
- *Crowdfunding*, i.e. asking many visitors to a website to make small donations for a project.

Some websites only display information, while others, such as *home banking*, *online shopping* and also *PayPal*, are more *interactive*, allowing you to transfer money between accounts and make *online payments* to other people.

The Creation of a Website

Many people will just use a Web browser to visit websites belonging to other people and organisations. However, if you have a small business or want to publicise a club or a community, say, then you may wish to obtain your own website.

Many websites are created by professional *Web designers*. It's also possible for the ordinary user to design their own website using apps or programs which include ready-made templates and designs to simplify the task.

Web Host

Web hosts are companies, including some *ISPs* (*Internet Service Providers*) who charge a monthly fee to store a website on their server, enabling other people to view it. The Web host can help you set up a *URL*, including a *domain name*, as discussed below.

URL

Every website has a unique address, known as a *URL* (*Uniform Resource Locator)* as shown below.

www.mywebsite.co.uk

Entering the URL into the address bar of a Web browser such as Google Chrome, Internet Explorer, Edge, Firefox or Safari displays the *Home page* of the website.

Domain Name

The part of the address to the right of **www.**, i.e. **mywebsite.co.uk** in the above example, is known as the *domain name*. You can make up your own domain name and register it with a specialist company, for a small annual fee. In the above example the *extension* **co** denotes a company website and **uk** is the country.

Web Pages

Web pages are written in a special language known as *HTML* or *Hypertext Markup Language*. Apart from HTML text, a Web page may contain *hyperlinks*, photos, diagrams, animations, sound and videos.

If you want to create your own website to share your latest news and photos with friends and family worldwide, you don't need to learn HTML. There are plenty of Web design programs such as *Wordpress* to simplify the task, including ready-made designs and *templates*.

Hyperlinks

Links or hyperlinks are a major feature of Web pages, allowing you to move to other Web pages or websites, while *browsing* or *surfing* the Web.

Links are *words* (often in blue text and underlined, as shown below) or *images* which can be selected (e.g. with a mouse) to move to another Web page.

View more photos
.

Web pages can also be created in Microsoft Word and Publisher, for example.

* If creating a Web page in Microsoft Word or Publisher, select or highlight the words or image to be used as the link.
* Then right click and select **Hyperlink** from the menu which appears, as shown below.

If you enter a page in a program like Microsoft Word or a Desktop Publishing program such as Microsoft Publisher, you can save it as a Web page using **Save As** from the **File** menu.

File name:	Latest news
Save as type:	Web Page (*.htm;*.html)

Once saved in the HTML format, the document is ready for *uploading* and saving or *publishing* on the website.

Publishing a Website in the Cloud

Uploading

This involves using an *FTP Client* to copy Web pages from a client computer up to a Web server, where they are saved. The pages are then accessible for *downloading* information to millions of users around the world.

FTP Client

A special program that uses a system known as *File Transfer Protocol* for uploading and downloading files over the Internet to and from a server. The FTP Client program may be part of the Web design software. Alternatively you can download a separate FTP Client from the Internet. Some of these are free.

Downloading

Using a Web browser to copy information (files, Web pages, etc.) from a Web server down to a *client* computer used by an individual, where it is saved on the Internal Storage such as hard drive or SSD.

Web Browser

The Web browser is at the centre of Cloud Computing. The browser provides the communication link between the client computer on our desk, or lap, etc., and the Web server, which may be on the other side of the world.

A browser is a program which allows you to display Web pages, after entering the URL for the website, as discussed on the previous page. Also to *browse* or move forwards and backwards between Web pages and to mark Web pages as *favourites* or *bookmarks* for future reference. Leading Web browsers are Google Chrome, Firefox, Internet Explorer Microsoft Edge, Safari and Opera.

Google   Apple   Microsoft   Internet   Mozilla   Opera
Chrome   Safari   Edge   Explorer   Firefox

New Windows PCs have Microsoft Edge and Internet Explorer, while Apple macBooks, iPads and iPhones have Safari. New Chromebooks and Android tablets and smartphones have Google Chrome. Chrome and Firefox can also be installed and set as the *default browser* on most other computers, replacing the pre-installed browser.

Google Chrome

Google Chrome is easily the most popular browser at the time of writing in 2019 with a worldwide market share of over 62%, followed by Safari on about 15%.

Google Chrome is also the basis of the Chrome OS (Operating System) used in Chromebooks. These are popular computers from major manufacturers, especially designed for Cloud Computing, as discussed on page 35.

Launching the Web Browser

Click or tap the icon for your browser, as shown on page 42. The browser opens displaying the *Home Page* as shown below. This example uses Google Chrome, but other browsers have very similar features, as shown on page 44.

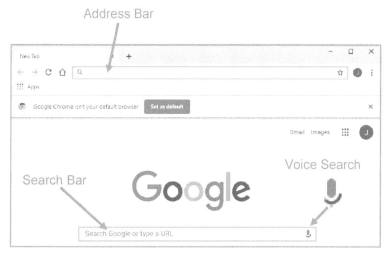

Chrome Home Page

As shown above, Chrome (and other browsers) have an *Address Bar* and a *Search Bar*. Both bars can be used for entering a *URL*, i.e. the address of a website. Both bars can also be used to enter a *keyword* to search for a particular subject. The Chrome *Address Bar* is also known as the *Omnibar*. The Search Bar can also be used to *speak* the keywords for a *voice search*. Searching for information by entering keywords is covered later in this chapter.

The next few pages describe accessing Web pages in the Cloud by entering a URL and then moving between pages using hyperlinks.

When you first open Chrome, **New Tab** is displayed at the top left of the screen, as shown below. *Tabs* are discussed in detail in Chapter 5.

Chrome

Google Chrome

As shown below, most of the other browsers have similar features to Google Chrome shown above.

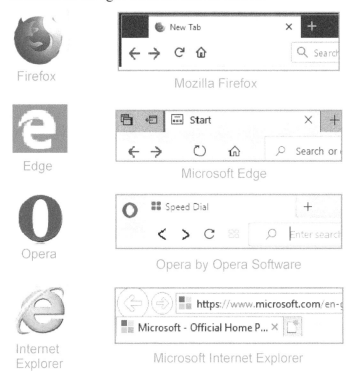

Firefox

Mozilla Firefox

Edge

Microsoft Edge

Opera

Opera by Opera Software

Internet Explorer

Microsoft Internet Explorer

Apple's Safari has similar browsing features but in quite a different layout, as discussed on page 54.

Opening a Website
1. Entering a URL

As shown on the previous page, most of the popular Web browsers have common features such as the Address Bar at the top left of the screen, as shown on pages 43 and 44.

Open or launch your browser, such as Chrome, Firefox, Edge, Internet Explorer, Opera, Safari, etc., by clicking or tapping its icon as shown on page 42 and 44.

Type a URL, i.e. Web address, such as **www.amazon.co.uk** into the Address Bar, as shown below in Chrome and press **Enter**. The Amazon website opens as shown below.

If you move the cursor around the screen, it changes from an arrow to a hand when it's over certain words, etc. These are clickable *links* or *hyperlinks* that take you to another Web page. Saving and revisiting Web pages using Favourites and Bookmarks, etc., is discussed in Chapter 5.

Some Useful Websites

The following Web addresses can be typed straight in after clicking in the Address Bar. There's no need to enter **www.** every time.

www.friendsreunited.com

Catch up with school friends.

.www.kelkoo.co.uk

Price checks on goods for sale.

www.moneysupermarket.com

Comparisons of prices of goods and services to help you save money.

www.thisismoney.co.uk

Guide to savings and loans.

www.uswitch.com

Look for cheapest gas, electricity and phone, etc.

www.flightradar24.com

Check on progress of airline flights around the world.

www.gov.uk/get-vehicle-information-from-dvla

Enter the registration number of a vehicle to find information such as the tax and MOT status and the technical specification.

www.direct.gov.uk

Guide to government services.

www.dwp.gov.uk

Advice on benefits, work and pensions.

2. The Keyword Search

As discussed previously, when you know the exact URL of a website, perhaps from an advertisement, etc., you can open the Home Page of the website directly by entering the URL in the Address Bar at the top of your browser, as shown on pages 43 and 44.

Alternatively you can search the Cloud for information on any conceivable subject, like using an incredibly powerful encyclopedia, but infinitely faster. This is done by typing or speaking *keywords* into the Search Bar in your browser, such as Chrome, Firefox, Edge, etc., as show below.

Or to carry out a *voice search*, tap the microphone icon shown on the right and below.

Search Google or type a URL

- Google is the most well-known *search engine*, i.e. program or app, and can be used with most browsers.
- Bing is the default search engine built into Microsoft Edge and is also used to power Yahoo!Search.

- Bing also allows you to search for an image or URL which you paste or drag onto a small window which pops up when you click the camera icon shown on the right and above.

After you've typed the keyword(s) and pressed **Enter**, a list of *search result*s including *links* to other *Web pages* is displayed. For example, to find out about a possible holiday destination, such as the island of **Madeira**, enter the name as the keyword in the Search Bar as shown below.

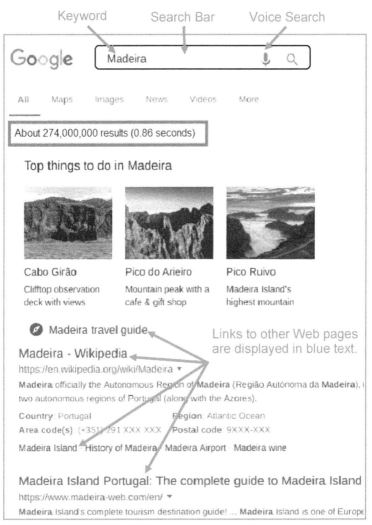

Narrowing Down a Search

As shown on the previous page, a staggering 274,000,000 pages were found containing the word Madeira. Many of these results may be irrelevant if you're just looking for the holiday island — you probably wouldn't be interested in Madeira cakes, for example.

So you need to narrow down the search by entering more keywords. As shown below, Google suggests some more searches at the bottom of each page of search results. Click on the links in blue text to visit Web pages of interest.

Searches related to madeira

madeira **funchai**	madeira **food**
madeira **beaches**	madeira **destinations**
madeira **weather**	madeira **climate**
madeira **hotels**	madeira **flights**

Eliminating Unwanted Search Results

Suppose you want to find out about all sorts of **owls** except **barn owls**. The word to be excluded, **barn** in this example, should be entered in the search bar, preceded by a minus sign, with *no space* in between, as shown below.

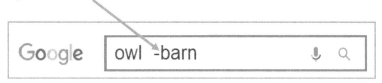

The above search produces a list of results involving owls of every type *other than* barn owls, e.g. little owl, long-eared owl, tawny owl and short-eared owl.

Crawling in the Cloud

Search engines such as Google use software known as *Web crawlers* to scan the billions of publicly available Web pages on the Internet. After following links and noting important words, any new or updated Web pages are added to the *Google Search Index*, containing over 100,000,000 gigabytes of data on Google's servers.

When you do a search, Google looks for Web pages containing your keywords and creates the results list. The Web pages most relevant to your search are placed at the top of the results list. Factors such as the frequency a Web page is visited and the number of links to it from other Web pages are used to *rank* the pages.

Some companies also pay to have their websites appear at the top of a list of search results. Others pay to have advertisements placed at the side of a list of search results.

Hyperscale Data Centres

When you consider the billions of Web pages, data files and software which make up the Cloud, it is perhaps not surprising that there are hundreds of data centres in America and around the world, belonging to companies such as Google, Amazon, Microsoft and IBM.

Hyperscale Data Centres are those containing more than 5000 Web servers or occupying more than 10,000 square feet. At the time of writing there are nearly 500 hyperscale data centres worldwide, with Microsoft alone having 45.

With the continuing shift towards Cloud Computing, the number of hyperscale data centres is expected to continue to grow.

Browsing in the Cloud

Introduction

The last chapter discussed the various Web browsers and how they can be used to access websites. If you know the address or *URL* of the site such as **www.mywebsite.co.uk** this can be typed into the browser's *Address Bar* to open the site immediately. If you don't know the address then you can search for a list of relevant sites after entering suitable *keywords* in the browser's *Search Bar*.

Once you have opened a website you can move about the Cloud to open different Web pages by clicking or tapping on *hyperlinks*. Moving around the Cloud in this way is referred to as *Web browsing* or *Surfing the Net*, the two terms often meaning the same thing.

Browsing vs Surfing

Strictly speaking, *Browsing* means to search for specific websites or information by entering a URL for a website or typing in relevant keywords to search for information. *Surfing* refers to moving around the Internet by aimlessly clicking or tapping *links* to see what appears next.

This chapter covers the following topics:

- Moving forward and back between Web pages.
- *Tabbed browsing*.
- The URL in detail.
- Revisiting Web pages using *Bookmarks/Favourites*.
- Viewing and clearing your *Browsing History*.
- Changing your *default Web browser*.

Starting to Browse

In an online shopping site like Amazon, the links take you to different departments or further details about a product, your account details or previous orders, as shown below.

Link or hyperlink

In the above example, as you pass the cursor over **Your Orders**, initially in black text, the words change to orange and are underlined. Click or tap the link Your Orders shown above to move to the Web page as shown on the tab below.

Tabbed Browsing

If you continue browsing or surfing the net, the name of the current Web page appears at the top of the tab. This has changed from **New Tab** on page 44 to **Your Orders** above and **Amazon UK Deals**, etc., shown on page 53.

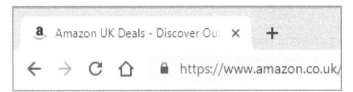

A tab allows you to switch between several open Web pages one at a time in a single Window, instead of on multiple windows on the screen. A tab might be used for a particular subject or website such as **amazon.co.uk** just described. As shown at the bottom of this page, you can have more than one tab displayed on the Tab Bar. The icons shown below are common to most browsers.

← →   Click or tap the arrows shown on the left to move forwards and backwards displaying each of the Web pages you've visited on the tab.

C   Click this icon to **Refresh** or **Reload** the latest version of a Web page, instead of an earlier version saved on a previous visit to the website.

⌂   Return to the Home Page of the browser, e.g. Chrome, Firefox, Microsoft Edge, etc.

×   Close the current tab.

+   Click to open a **New Tab**. When you open another Web page in the **New Tab**, its name appears highlighted at the top of the tab as shown below.

Tabs in Tab Bar

Corresponding icons for the Apple Safari browser are shown on page 54.

Safari

Tap the Safari icon shown on the right to open the Safari Home Page. Shown below is the top of the Safari browser used on Apple iPads and iPhones, etc. Although the layout is different from the browsers shown on page 44, the basic functions are very similar, as discussed below.

Safari

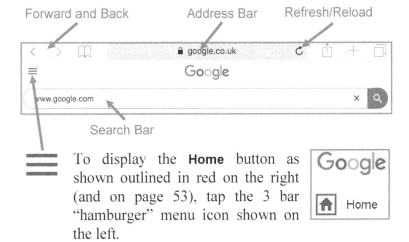

Forward and Back   Address Bar   Refresh/Reload

Search Bar

To display the **Home** button as shown outlined in red on the right (and on page 53), tap the 3 bar "hamburger" menu icon shown on the left.

Tabbed Browsing

Safari on the iPad and iPhone has a *Tab Bar* across the top of the screen, as shown below.

Tabs icon

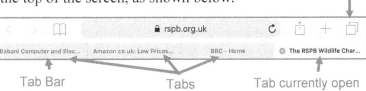

Tab Bar   Tabs   Tab currently open

- If necessary, to display the Tab Bar, tap the **Settings** icon shown on the right, then scroll down and select **Safari**.

- Tap the **Show Tab Bar** button to switch the Tab Bar On, as shown in green on the right below.

- The Tab Bar should now be displayed as shown near the bottom of page 54.

- As you open new Web pages they are attached to the currently open tab and the name of the new page is shown on the tab. The currently open tab is highlighted in white as shown for the **RSPB** site near the botton of page 54 on the right.

- To open a new tab *tap and hold* the **Tabs** icon shown on the right and on page 54.

- Select New Tab from the menu which is displayed. The next website you open will appear in its own new tab.

- To view thumbnail images of all the tabs currently open, as shown below, briefly tap the **Tabs** icon shown again on the right.

- Click the cross to close a tab, as shown below left.

Close Tab

- To open a recently closed tab *tap and hold* the + icon shown on the right and on page 54. Then select the tab from the list.

The URL in More Detail

To enter a URL into the Address Bar, simply type the *domain* part of the URL, i.e. after **www.**, then press **Enter**. **https://www.** shown below is added automatically.

http

Some websites use *http* rather than *https* shown above. **http** stands for *hypertext transfer protocol*. Hypertext allows *hyperlinks* or *links* to other web pages, etc., to be inserted.

https

The **s** in **https** above refers to a *secure website*, used for sending and receiving important data in activities such as online banking and shopping. Data moving between your computer and a secure website is *encrypted* or *scrambled* and can only be read by users who have a *private key*.

 This icon in front of a URL shows that the website has a *security certificate* from a *Certification Authority*.

IP Address

Whereas the URL is the address of a *website*, the *IP* (*Internet Protocol*) *address* identifies a *computer* on the Internet, e.g.**192.68.1.139**. This allows the computer to send and receive data on a *TCP/IP* network. *TCP* (*Transmission Control Protocol*) is a set of rules for the sending and receiving of data on a computer network.

Revisiting Web Pages

Bookmarks and Favourites

To revisit a Web page in the future with a single tap or click, you can save it in a list as a *Bookmark* or a *Favourite*. These are essentially the same.

Chrome, Firefox and Opera use Bookmarks while Internet Explorer and Edge use Favourites (spelt as Favorite in American English). Safari uses both Favourites and Bookmarks.

Your Browsing History

This is a list of the Web pages that you've visited. The *History* list is recorded automatically. This saves you typing the Web address in again if you want to revisit the site. A website you've entered may have needed a password and other personal information and this is also saved.

The Web Cache

When a Web page is opened in your browser for the first time, a temporary copy of the page is saved in an area of your hard drive or SSD known as the *cache*. Next time you access the Web page it opens much faster. The page recovered from the cache may not always be the latest version. Click or tap the **Refresh** button shown on the right and on page 53 to display the latest version of a Web page, including any updates since your last visit.

Your Reading List

Some Web browsers such as Safari, Firefox and Edge provide a *Reading List* where you can save Web pages to read later, perhaps offline. Once you've finished with the page it can be deleted from your Reading List.

Saving Bookmarks and Favourites

Google Chrome

When you open a Web page and then decide to mark it as a bookmark or favourite, tap the icon shown on the right, which normally appears near to the top right-hand corner of the screen, as shown below using the Chrome Browser.

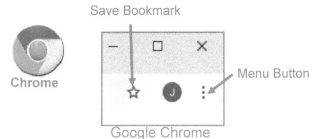

A small window opens as shown below, allowing you to change the name of the bookmark if you wish.

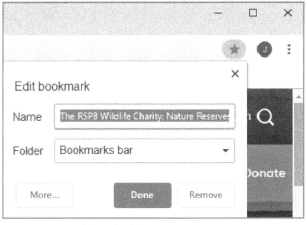

Google Chrome

Finally click **Done** to save the bookmark.

As shown below, other popular browsers such as Firefox, Microsoft Edge and Internet Explorer have an icon near the top right of the screen, for saving the current Web page in the list of bookmarks or favourites.

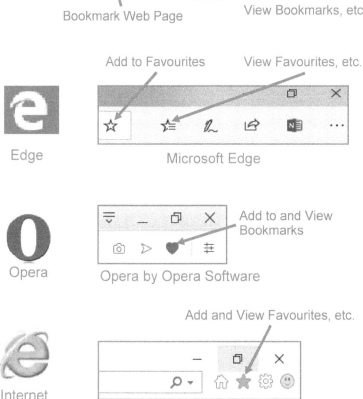

Firefox

Firefox

Bookmark Web Page

View Bookmarks, etc.

Add to Favourites

View Favourites, etc.

Edge

Microsoft Edge

Add to and View Bookmarks

Opera

Opera by Opera Software

Add and View Favourites, etc.

Internet Explorer

Internet Explorer

Managing Bookmarks and Favourites

As mentioned earlier, bookmarks and favourites are essentially the same thing. Both words are used to mean lists of websites you save to view in the future. These normally appear along a horizontal *Bookmarks Bar* or *Favourites Bar* or in a vertical list.

Chrome Browser

For example, in the Chrome browser, click or tap the 3-dot menu at the top right of the screen. Then tap **Bookmarks**, as shown below on the right. A second menu opens in the left-hand panel as shown below, including the list of bookmarked Web pages.

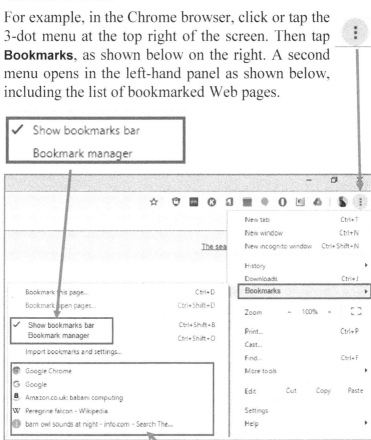

List of Bookmarked Web Pages

If you click or tap **Show bookmarks bar**, as shown on the previous page, the names of the bookmarked Web pages appear across the top of the screen, as shown below.

Chrome Bookmarks Bar

Deleting a Bookmark or Favourite

Right click or tap and hold the bookmark or favourite and select **Delete** from the menu which appears. On some mobile devices tap the 3-dot menu at the side of each bookmark to display the menu including the **Delete** option.

Firefox, Edge, Opera and Internet Explorer Browsers

The methods for viewing and deleting bookmarks and favourites are basically very similar for the other browsers listed on page 59. Simply click or tap the icon to **View Bookmarks** (or **View Favourites**) shown on page 59 then follow the menus, similar to the Chrome menus shown on page 60. One difference is that the heart shaped **Bookmarks** menu icon on Opera appears on a menu bar down left-hand side of the screen, as shown here on the right.

Safari Browser

Saving Bookmarks and Favourites

Safari

- With Safari open at the Web page you want to view in future, tap the icon shown on the right and below.

- Select either **Add Bookmark** or **Add to Favourites** shown below.

- Then select **Save** to add the website to either the **Bookmarks** or **Favourites** list, shown on the next page.

Viewing Bookmarks and Favourites

- Tap the book icon shown on the right and at the top left of this page.

- The **Bookmarks** list opens as shown on the next page.

- You can also select **Bookmarks Bar** shown on the next page to view the bookmarks across the screen.

- Alternatively select and view the **Favourites** list and the **Favourites Bar**. The **Favourites Bar**, when switched On is displayed across the top of the screen.

nrssgsfrfsfnrmprpsrrfsfr

ssssrsrsrrsrp

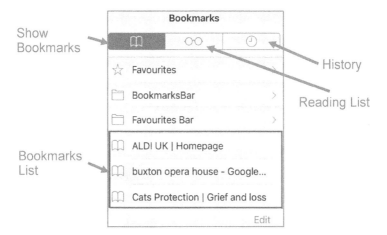

- If necessary the **Favourites Bar** can be switched on after tapping the **Settings** icon, then scrolling down to **Safari** and tapping the button, which should be green as shown on the right below.

Deleting Bookmarks and Favourites

- Tap Edit as shown above at the bottom of the **Bookmarks** or **Favourite** list and then tap the – sign which appears in a red circle against each item.

- Finally tap **Delete** and **Done** to remove the Bookmark or Favourite.

- The **History** and **Reading List** shown at the top of this page are discussed elsewhere in this chapter.

Your Browsing Data

Your Browsing History

The *History* feature is a list of the websites you've visited, created automatically by the Web browser.

Advantages of the History list:

- Revisiting a Web page by simply clicking or tapping its entry in the list.
- A parent, grandparent or teacher can monitor what children have been looking at.

Disadvantages of the History list:

- The History list may take up precious storage space.
- Most browsers have a *Privacy Mode* or *Incognito Mode* in **Settings**, to switch on *Private Browsing*. In this mode your History list and other browsing information is not saved at the end of a session. So other people with access to your computer will not be able to see what you've been doing.

Cookies

- *Cookies* are small files saved by websites, recording your personal details and browsing habits. This saves time when revisiting a website, but cookies are also used to help target advertising at potential customers.

Cached Data

- *Cached data* includes copies of Web pages temporarily saved on your Internal Storage. This speeds up the revisiting of a website.

It's a good idea to clear your browsing data from time to time, especially on the latest slimline Cloud-ready laptops. These include Google Chromebooks and also laptops running the cut-down Windows 10 S version. These have low Internal Storage capacity on SSDs.

Clearing Browsing Data
Chrome Browser

- Select the 3-dot menu button at the top of the screen.
- From the menu select **More tools** and then **Clear browsing data...** to open the window shown below.

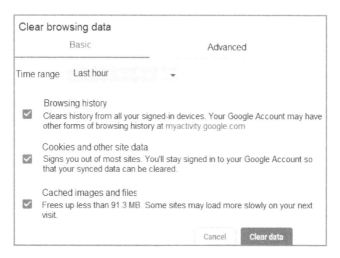

- Select the **Time range** for which the data is to be removed, ranging from **Last hour**, **Last 24 hours**, **Last 7 days**, **Last 4 weeks** to **All time**.
- Select with a tick the data to be deleted and then select **Clear data** shown above.

Android smartphones and tablets using Chrome and Firefox use a similar method to clear browsing data, as follows:

- Select the 3-dot button at the top right of the screen.
- Select **History** then **Clear browsing data...**.
- Select the **Time range** and clear the data as described above.

Clearing Browsing Data
Firefox, Edge and Opera Browsers

The general method for these browsers is as follows:

- Select the menu button, usually at the top right of the screen, as shown below, outlined in red.

Firefox   Edge   Opera

- Select **History**.
- Select **Clear History** or **Clear Browsing** data.
- Select the time period and data to be removed, i.e. **History, Cookies, Cache**.

Internet Explorer Browser

- Select the **Tools** icon outlined in red on the right.
- Select **Safety**.
- Select **Delete browsing history**....

Internet Explorer

Safari Browser

- Select the book icon shown on the right then select the clock icon to open the **History** list.

- Select **Clear** at the bottom of the **History** list then select the time period and tap **Clear** to remove your browsing data.

The Default Web Browser

The Web browser is, to mix metaphors, the packhorse of Cloud Computing. It is used to upload and download all of your data and requests for information to and from the Cloud. So it's vital that you're happy with your browser.

The main computer operating systems all pre-install their own *default Web browser* on a new computer. The default browser is the one automatically used to open a Web page.

- Microsoft install Edge as the default browser on Windows 10, with Internet Explorer also still present.
- Apple provide Safari on iPads, iPhones, Macs, etc.
- Google build Chrome into all the Android tablets and smartphones and the Cloud-based Chromebook.

In addition to the above pre-installed browsers you may wish to try popular alternatives such as Mozilla Firefox and Opera, which can be easily installed on all the main computer platforms. Chrome can also be widely used.

Installing a New Browser

- Firefox, Opera and Chrome can be installed from the Google Play Store and the Apple App Store.
- Otherwise enter the name of the browser into Google to open the browser's website. Then click or tap the **Download** button to install the browser.
- When you click or tap to run the new browser you are asked to agree to make it your default browser.

| Use Firefox as my default browser | Not now |

| Would you like to make Opera your everyday browser? | Yes, set it as default browser |

Changing Your Default Browser

Listed below are some alternative ways of making one of your other installed browsers your default browser.

Windows 10

- Select the **Settings** icon, shown right, on the Start Menu then select **Apps** and **Default apps**.
- Then select **Microsoft Edge** to display the alternative browsers shown below on the left.

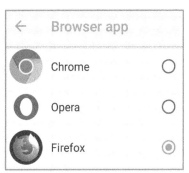

Windows 10   Android

- Then click the browser which is to replace Microsoft Edge as your default browser.

Android and Chromebook Computers

- On Android devices, select **Settings**, **Apps & notifications**, **Advanced**, **Default Apps**, **Browser app** and switch on the required default browser, as shown on the right above.

Apple iPads, etc.

- Apple don't allow you to replace Safari as your default browser. However, you can still install another browser and use it after tapping its icon.

Google Drive

Introduction

The next few chapters cover three of the main Cloud Storage Systems, namely Google Drive, Microsoft OneDrive and Dropbox from Dropbox, Inc.

Drive OneDrive Dropbox

These systems provide storage space for your files, such as documents, photos and videos and are available for all types of computer - desktop, laptop, tablet and smartphone.

As discussed elsewhere in this book, you can easily run out of file storage space on your device. This is especially true on smartphones and tablets. Also slimline laptops such as Chromebooks and Windows 10 S Cloudbooks are designed to use the Cloud rather than the storage on the device.

With all of the above systems, an initial amount of Cloud Storage is provided free and more is available for a monthly subscription, as discussed shortly. Then your data files and photos, etc., can be viewed on any computer connected to the Internet, anywhere in the world.

As well as providing storage space for data, Google Drive and OneDrive include *Web-based apps* for important office tasks such as word processing and spreadsheets, as discussed on page 71 and in more detail in Chapter 12.

Google Drive Cloud Storage

Files are stored *online* in a folder called My Drive within Google Drive and this resides in a Web server in a data centre which could be anywhere in the world, as discussed in Chapter 3.

Google Sync, automatically *synchronizes* files from the Drive website to every computer, tablet or smartphone you are signed into with a Google account. Also, as discussed shortly, if you take photos on your smartphone while travelling anywhere, they can be immediately uploaded to Drive on the Web and viewable on any desktop computer, laptop or tablet anywhere.

Similarly data files created on one computer, can be viewed and edited on another computer including mobile devices when travelling.

Google Drive lets you *upload* files from a plug-in storage device such as a flash drive/memory stick as discussed in Chapter 13.

Signing up for a free Google Drive account, as discussed shortly, gives you 15GB of free storage or you can pay £1.59 a month for 100GB (Gigabytes) or £7.99 a month for 1TB (Terabyte). Gigabytes and Terabytes are discussed on pages 7 and 174. Purchasers of the Google Chromebook discussed on page 35 can claim 100GB of free Google Drive storage for two years. 1GB can store very roughly 300-1000 photos taken on a smartphone. (Photos taken on a DSLR camera can be much bigger).

While Google Drive allows files and documents to be synced and viewed on all types of computer, tablet or smartphone, *Backup and Sync* is a relatively new feature which provides extra features on PCs and Macs, as discussed in Chapter 7.

Online or Web-based Apps

As mentioned earlier, Google Drive includes several *online* or *web-based* apps. All you need to run these apps is a Web browser such as Google Chrome, Firefox, or Edge, etc. Although the apps are displayed in the Web browser on your screen while running, the *program execution* takes place on a Web server computer in a remote data centre.

The Web-based apps in Drive are free and include the Docs word processor, the Sheets speadsheet and the Slides presentation app, similar to the Microsoft Office suite. The Drive apps can also be used to open and edit files created in MS Word and Excel, etc. Although simple to use, Docs, Sheets and Slides have all the text formatting and other features needed for many home and office tasks, as shown below, and are now very widely used in large organisations.

Google Docs Menu Bar

Most users only require a fraction of the many sophisticated features in Microsoft Office. While Microsoft Office 365 requires a monthly fee, the Internet-only Microsoft *Office Online* provides free, basic versions of Word, Excel, and PowerPoint. Office 365 can be used both offline and online. Software traditionally stored on your hard drive can be very expensive and when new versions are developed they may not be compatible with an older computer. Cloud-based software is managed and updated by professional staff and is independent of your computer — the Web browser simply manages the input and output between your client computer and the Web server at the data centre.

Setting Up Google Drive

(Installing the latest Backup and Sync for Windows PCs and Macs is discussed in Chapter 7).

If Drive is already installed on your computer, tablet or smartphone, its icon will appear on your apps screen or desktop, as shown on the right and below on an Android smartphone.

If you can't find the Drive icon, the app can easily be installed from the app store for your computer. Alternatively, on all types of computer, visit the Drive website at:

www.google.com/drive

Then click or tap **Download Google Drive** shown below to download and install the Drive app.

Creating a Google Account (All Devices)

As shown below, a Google Account can be used to access a wide range of Google apps, apart from Google Drive.

- Tap the Drive icon shown on the previous page.
- If you have a Google Account, sign in as shown below, unless you are already signed in.
- If you don't yet have a Google Account, select Create account as shown below and click or tap **Next**.

The **Google Sign in** window shown on the previous page is used on all types of computers, smartphones and tablets and can also be accessed using the following general method:

- Click or tap the relevant icon shown below to open the **Settings** menu.

Windows   Android   iPad/iPhone

- From the **Settings** menu select:

    Accounts > Add an account > Google

- This opens the **Sign in** window shown on the previous page. Select Create account to open the **Create your Google Account** window shown below.

Enter your name and username and password and other personal details.

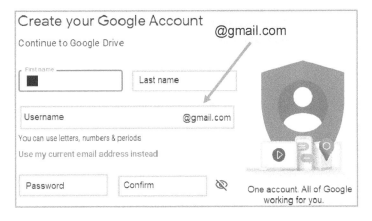

- Google Account usernames usually end in **@gmail.com**, already inserted by the software as shown above — you don't need to type it.

Google Drive Locations

Google Drive, launched in 2012, is basically a file storage system. However, the term Google Drive refers to several related features in the overall process, as follows:

- It is an *app* on mobile devices for uploading files to the Cloud and syncing, i.e. *mirroring*, them to every other computer you sign into with a Google Account.

- Google Drive creates a *folder* for all your files on the Internal Storage on Windows PCs and Apple Macs.

- On Windows 10 the **Google Drive** folder appears in the **Quick access** list at the top left of the File Explorer as shown below:

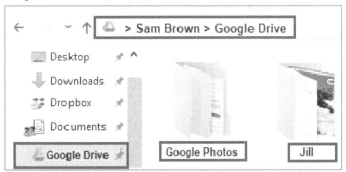

- The same files and folders are saved on the hard drive **OS(C:)** in your **Users** folder, as shown below.

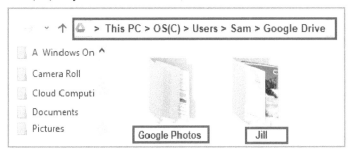

- As shown below, the same files and folders are also displayed in **My Drive** on the **Drive** *website* at:

drive.google.com

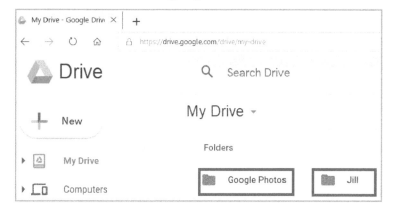

- The website for Google Photos can be displayed in a Web browser after entering the following:

photos.google.com

Uploading Files to Google Drive
Windows PC, Mac, Google Chromebook

- Open the website at **drive. google.com** and select **New** at the top left-hand side, as shown on the left below.

The menu on the right above has options to :

- Create a new **Folder** within the My Drive folder.

- Select either **File** or **Folder upload** to copy a file or folder from your Internal Storage such as a hard drive/SSD or a USB device such as a flash drive or an external hard drive/SSD as discussed in Chapter 13.

- Then select the required file or folder to upload to My Drive from the file manager, such as Windows 10 File Explorer, which opens on the screen.

- Click **Open** to upload a file or **Upload** to upload a folder and save it in My Drive. It can now be viewed at **drive.google.com** on any computer connected to the Internet and signed in to your Google Account.

- You can also *drag and drop* files and folders from an external device such as a flash drive or SD card to the My Drive folder using a mouse in Windows File Explorer. In the Chromebook Files app you can use two fingers or a mouse to drag and drop.

- Tap the icon for Google Drive on the Apps screen, as shown on the right.
- Tap the **+** icon at the lower right of the screen to open the **Create new** menu shown below.
- Select **Upload** from the menu shown below.

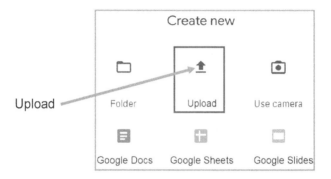

- The **Upload** list opens as shown on the right for Androids. Devices outlined in red are a **KINGSTON** flash drive, a **maxone** external hard drive and an SD card in a card reader, labelled as **USB drive**. These USB devices were connected by an OTG cable as discussed in Chapter 13.

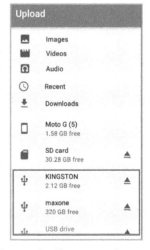

- Browse the list and then tap the required file or folder to upload it to My Drive. Files and folders can be uploaded in a similar way from some, but not all, iPads and iPhones.

Google Backup and Sync

Introduction

The last few pages described the **Upload** option used to manually select and copy a file or folder from your computer, tablet or smartphone to the My Drive folder in Google Drive in the Cloud. This is useful, for example, if someone gives you some files on a USB flash drive or SD card and you want to copy them up to Google Drive.

Backup and Sync

Windows PC and Mac

- Backup and Sync, launched in 2017, is an app which *continuously* backs up *selected* files and folders from your hard drive or USB devices to Google Drive in the Cloud.

- Selected backed up files can be downloaded from My Drive in the Cloud and saved on the Internal Storage of any computers you are signed into.

- Windows 10 S Cloudbooks can only use apps from the Microsoft Store, which doesn't include Backup and Sync. Cloudbook users can switch, *irreversibly*, to Windows 10 Home and then run Backup and Sync.

Other Computers

- Mobile devices — Android and iPads, etc., have a photos Backup and Sync app within Google Photos.

- Chromebooks don't have a Backup and Sync app but you can use the Files App to drag files up to Google Drive from where they are synced to your other devices.

Installing Backup and Sync

The following pages describe the setting up and use of Backup and Sync on a Windows PC. The methods used on Mac computers are broadly similar.

- Click the Windows **Start** icon shown on the right to display the list of apps installed on your computer.

- If the Backup and Sync app is already installed on your computer, it will be listed as shown below.

- If it's necessary to install Backup and Sync, first launch your Web browser such as Chrome, Firefox or Edge and open the website:

drive.google.com

- Click the **Settings** gear icon shown on the right and below and then select **Get Backup and Sync for Windows** from the menu.

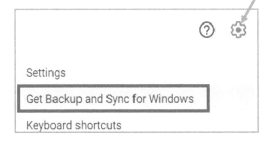

- The **Download Google Drive** Web page opens with download options for **Personal** and **Business** use.

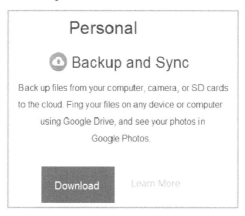

- Select **Download** under **Personal**, as shown above, then click **Agree and download** and then wait a few minutes while Backup and Sync is downloaded.

- Click **installbackupandsync.exe** which appears in the bottom left-hand corner of the screen then click **Run** to install **Backup and Sync**.

- You are then informed that the installation is complete and **Backup and Sync from Google** will be listed in the **Start** menu, as shown below, after clicking the Windows icon.

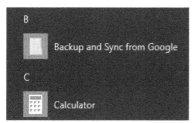

- After the installation, an icon for Backup and Sync app appears on the Taskbar at the bottom right of the screen, as shown below.

- Clicking this icon allows you to monitor the syncing activities of Backup and Sync, as shown on page 88. On a new installation of Backup and Sync you are required to sign in with an existing Google Account, or create a new one, as discussed on pages 73 and 74.

- If you already have a Google Account click **Sign in** as shown above then enter the email address or phone number of your Google Account and click **Next**, as shown on page 73.

- Alternatively click Create account shown on page 73 and enter your name and email address, as discussed on page 74.

- You are then asked to choose the folders from your computer to continuously back up to Google Drive, as shown on the next page.

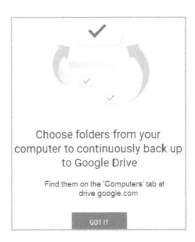

- Click **GOT IT** shown above. This displays the Window shown on page 84, which allows you to select which folders to back up from your computer to Google Drive in the Cloud.

- Click **CHOOSE FOLDER** outlined in red on page 84 then select the folders to be uploaded to Drive from the File Explorer which opens. This can include files and folders stored on USB devices plugged into your computer and SD cards as discussed in Chapter 13.

- Select either **High-quality** photos for free unlimited storage or select **Original quality** that counts against your Drive storage allowance, discussed on page 70.

Photo and video upload size Learn more

◉ High quality (free unlimited storage)
Great visual quality at a reduced file size

○ Original quality (103.7 GB storage left)
Full resolution that counts against your quota

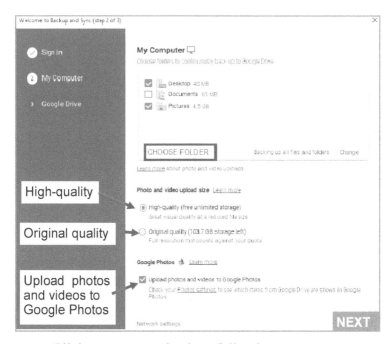

- Click **NEXT** and the following screen appears. Click **GOT IT** to open the window shown at the top of the next page.

- As shown above, this allows you to sync folders from My Drive in the Cloud to the local storage on your computer, such as a hard drive or SSD.

- If you have limited local storage, you may need to select **Sync these folders only...** to tick the folders to sync to your local storage drive, etc., as shown on page 87.

- Click **START** shown above to begin syncing your files.

The Backup and Sync Menu

- After the initial setting up process just described, you can change the settings at any time after clicking the Backup and Sync icon on the Windows Taskbar shown on the right and on page 82.

- Then click the 3-dot menu button and select **Preferences** from the pop-up menu shown at the top of page 86.

·

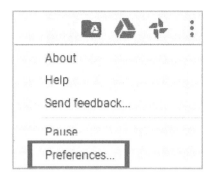

The **Preferences-Backup and Sync** window opens, as shown below, allowing you to select which files are to be backed up from My Computer to Google Drive in the Cloud. This is very similar to the **Welcome** window shown on page 84 in the Backup and Sync setting up process.

Google Drive

Removing items

Upload new photos to Google Photos

- At the bottom of the window on page 86 is a check box to **Upload newly added photos and videos to Google Photos**, as shown below.

- Click USB devices & SD cards shown above to add removable storage devices to Backup and Sync.

- Select **Google Drive** outlined in red on page 86 to open a window as shown below. This is similar to that shown at the top of page 85, allowing you to sync My Drive to the hard drive, etc., on your computer.

- Then select either **Sync everything in My Drive** or **Sync these folders only...** and tick the folders you wish to sync to the local storage. Syncing everything might be a problem if your Internal Storage is low.

Viewing Your Files and Folders

- Click the Backup and Sync icon on the Taskbar to open the window shown below.

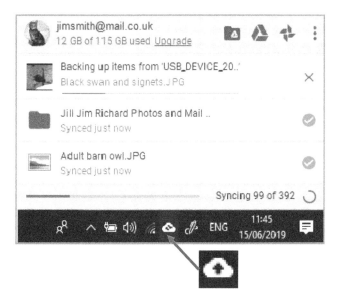

As shown above, this displays the continuous process of backing up and syncing files and folders. The icons at the top right above have the following functions:

 Open the menu shown at the top of page 86.

 Display Google Photos in its website at:
photos. google.com

 Display Google Drive in its website at:
drive. google.com

 Open the Google Drive folder in the File Explorer.

Inserting a Taskbar Icon for the Google Drive Folder

To place an icon on the Taskbar:

- Display **Backup and Sync from Google** on the Start Menu as shown below and on page 80.

- Right click over the **Backup and Sync...** shown above then click **More** and select **Pin to taskbar**.

- Click the new Taskbar icon as shown on the right, at any time, to quickly open the Google Drive folder, as shown on page 75.

The Computers Folder in Google Drive

- Display the **Drive** website shown below, as described near the bottom of page 88.

- Double-click **Computers** outlined in red below.

- This shows your computers and external USB devices such as flash drives.

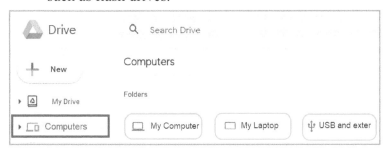

- Double-click a name such as **My Computer** to show all the folders that have been backed up and synced from that computer or USB device.

Deleting Files and Folders

As discussed elsewhere, Backup and Sync means that changes you make on one computer are quickly applied to all the computers you are signed into. Depending on your settings, one possible problem may occur if you accidentally delete a file or folder on Google Drive in the Cloud or from the Internal Storage of one of your computers.

Then Backup and Sync might delete all copies of the file or folder from the Internal Storage such as hard drives and SSDs on all of your other computers.

For example, accidentally deleting every copy of photos or videos of an important family event. Fortunately Backup and Sync has settings to prevent such a disaster:

- Select the Backup and Sync app shown on the right and page 88.

- Select **Preferences** from the menu shown on page 86 to open the **Preferences** window, also shown on page 86.

- Under **Removing items** shown below and on page 86, click the arrowhead shown below on the lower right.

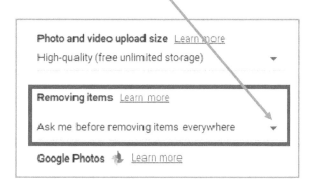

The following menu appears:

Remove items everywhere

Don't remove items everywhere

Ask me before removing items everywhere

- Select either **Don't remove items everywhere** or **Ask me before deleting items everywhere**.

- Your chosen option will then appear under **Removing items**, replacing the previous setting shown on pages 86 and 90.

Removing items Learn more

Don't remove items everywhere   ▼

Restoring Deleted Files

- Windows 10 sends deleted files to a **Recycle Bin**. This can be opened in the File Explorer by double-clicking its icon on the Windows 10 Desktop.

- Deleted files can be restored to their original location for up to 90 days.

- As shown above, there is an option to empty the recycle bin to free up space on the hard drive, etc.

Backup and Sync in the Photos App
Android Smartphones and Tablets, iPads and iPhones

As discussed earlier, Backup and Sync on Windows and Macs can copy some or all of your Google Drive folders and files *of all types* to your local storage on your hard drive or SSD. Mobile computers such as Androids, iPads and iPhones have very limited Internal Storage on their SSDs or eMMCs. Similarly Chromebooks and Windows 10 S Cloudbooks have much less Internal Storage than PCs and Macs since they are designed to use mainly Cloud storage. So syncing files down to these Cloud-ready devices could quickly fill their limited storage.

However, there is a version of Backup and Sync for your photos within the Google Photos app on Androids and iPad, etc. When you're connected to the Internet, any photos and videos taken on your smartphone or tablet are:

- Backed up to your Google Photos website in the Cloud.

- Accessible from any other computer you are signed into with a Google Account.

- Depending on your settings, as discussed on page 87, any new photos and videos taken on your phone may be downloaded to the Internal Storage on your other computers.

- Setting up Backup and Sync described on page 93 is the same for Androids and iPads and iPhones.

Setting Up Backup and Sync in the Photos App
Android Smartphones and Tablets, iPads and iPhones

- If necessary, install the Google Photos app from your App Store.

- Tap the Google Photos icon on your Apps screen.

- Tap the 3-bar "hamburger" menu icon shown on the right, at the top left of the screen.

- Make sure you are signed in to your Google Account at the top of the screen, as shown below.

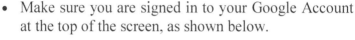

- Select **Settings** on the menu.

- Select **Backup & sync** shown above and, if necessary, make sure it is **On** as shown in blue below.

- There is also an option to delete photos and videos once they have been backed up, as outlined in red above.

Alternatives to Backup and Sync

Files and folders can be *dragged and dropped* or *copied and pasted* from the Internal Storage such as a hard drive or a USB device to the Google Drive folder, using the Windows File Explorer as shown on page 75.

As discussed in Chapter 6, files and folders can also be imported to Google Drive using the Upload tool on the Google Drive website. Once in the Google Drive folder in the Cloud, the files and folders are synced to all the other computers, etc., that you are signed into.

Chromebooks

Perhaps surprisingly, the Google Backup and Sync app is not available for the Google Chromebook. Chromebooks have very limited Internal Storage, known as the **Downloads** folder. This is located within the Files App, as shown on the next page. Backup and Sync *continuously* downloads files from Google Drive to the local storage. This would not be practical with the limited storage of the **Downloads** folder. Similarly with Windows 10 S Cloudbooks.

However, Chromebooks (and also Windows 10 S Cloudbooks) do have two full size USB ports into which you can insert USB devices such as flash drives, SD cards and external hard drives and SSDs as discussed in Chapter 13. These can be used to import files to **Google Drive** as discussed below. Then they are synced to all of your other computers. using a Google Chromebook.

- Select the Google Photos app on the Chromebook All Apps screen.

- Tap or click the 3-bar "hamburger" menu icon at the top left of the screen.

- Select **Settings** on the menu.

- Make sure **Sync photos & videos from Google Drive** is turned on as shown in blue below.

Google Drive
Sync photos & videos from Google Drive. Learn more.

- Plug any external devices into one of the USB ports. Tap or click the Files App icon.

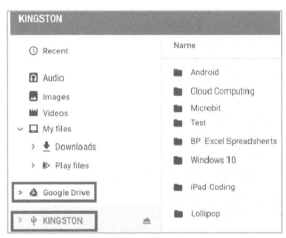

- Drag and drop or copy and paste any files or folders from the external device to **Google Drive**, shown above. In the above example, the external device is a **KINGSTON** USB flash drive.

Flash drives and SD cards, discussed in Chapter 13, with capacities of up to 128GB, are readily available. These can be used as *extra storage* to supplement the limited storage on Cloud-ready Chromebooks, Cloudbooks, tablets and smartphones. External storage can also be used as *secure backups* for files such as photos. Drag and drop or copy and paste files from Google Drive.

Google Drive is Still Alive

- As discussed in the last two chapters, Google Drive is one of the leading Cloud Storage Systems.

- Originally there was a Google Drive *app* for all of the main types of computer, tablet and smartphone.

- The Google Drive app has been replaced on PCs and Macs by the new *Backup and Sync* app. This allows you to *select* files to be *continuously* backed up to the Cloud and *synced* to all your computers.

- Google Drive is still accessible to all types of computer in the form of the Google Drive and Google Photos websites. Also the Google Drive folder on the Internal Storage on PCs and Macs and the Google Drive App on Androids, iPads and iPhones.

- Files such as documents, photos and videos can be *uploaded* to the Drive and Photos *websites* from your hard drive/SSD or from external USB devices. Files on the Drive and Photos websites can be viewed on any Internet computer you are signed into.

- Copies of files may be *downloaded* or *synced* to the Internal Storage on all of your computers. Changes made to a file on one computer are synced to the copies of the same files on your other computers.

- File synchronisation can result in the accidental deletion of every copy of a file from the Cloud and from the storage on all of your computers. Settings exist to prevent this. (Please see pages 90 and 91).

- For important files such as irreplaceable photos and videos, backing up to separate, removable storage such as a USB flash drive is recommended.

Managing Google Drive

Introduction

PCs and Macs

As discussed in the previous chapters, a Googe Drive folder for storing your files, such as documents and photos, is created on Windows PCs and Macs on the Internal Storage, such as the hard drive or SSD. Access is also provided to your files via the Google Drive and Photos websites.

Files can be dragged and dropped into the Google Drive Folder using the File Explorer and then *uploaded* automatically to the Drive and Photos websites. Or use the **Upload** option in the Drive and Photos websites.

Android and iOS Tablets and Smartphones

Mobile devices such as Android and iOS (Apple) tablets and smartphones have very limited Internal Storage, compared with desktop computers and larger laptops. So they don't have a Google Drive folder on the device itself. Instead they use the Google Drive and Google Photos apps to access files and folders on the Drive and Photos websites. So they normally need an Internet connection.

However, if you wish to access files *offline*, it is possible to *download* individual files to local storage such as the SSD or eMMC used on mobile devices, or the external storage devices discussed in Chapter 13. Obviously care must be taken to avoid using up the limited Internal Storage space available on an SSD or eMMC on a tablet or smartphone.

This chapter discusses maintenance tasks such as creating folders and moving and deleting files and folders within the Google Drive folder and the Drive and Photos websites.

Windows PC

Creating a Folder in the Drive Folder

You can create your own folders and sub-folders within the Google Drive folder as follows:

- Click the File Explorer icon, shown on the right, on the Taskbar or on the Start Menu and select **Google Drive** near the top of the left-hand panel under **Quick access**.

- If necessary select the required sub-folder within the Google Drive folder.

- Select **New folder** from the menu bar across the top of the File Explorer screen.

- Replace **New folder** with a meaningful name and press **Enter**.

Saving and Moving Files and Folders

- Files can be saved in a selected folder using the **File/ Save As** option in an app such as a word processor or spreadsheet, etc.

- Files and folders can also be moved and saved in a folder by *dragging and dropping* in the File Explorer, using a mouse.

- Or by using **Cut** or **Copy** from the menus shown on the next page which pop up after *right-clicking* over the relevant file or folder to be moved or copied.

- Then *right-clicking* over the destination folder and selecting **Paste** from the pop-up menu shown on the right on the next page.

Windows PC

Managing Files and Folders in the Drive Folder

- Right-clicking over a file or folder in the Windows File Explorer opens either the file or folder menu shown below.

- The **Paste** option appears on the folder menu after a file or folder has been cut or copied to the *clipboard* temporary memory.

File menu

Folder menu

- **Restore previous versions** shown above may be useful, perhaps to revert to the original version or to track changes in a document or report.

- The **Delete** option is discussed on page 101.

Windows PC

Managing Files on the Drive Website

- New folders can be created on the Google Drive website as discussed on page 77.

- Right-click over a file or folder on the website to open a menu. The file menu is shown below and the folder menu is very similar.

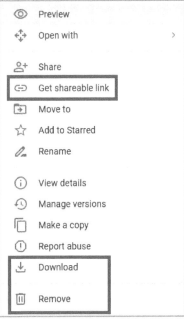

Drive website file menu

- **Download** allows you to copy a file or folder to your local hard drive/SSD or to a removable storage device such as a flash drive, etc., as discussed in Chapter 13.

- **Remove** is discussed on the next page.

- **Get shareable link** is discussed shortly.

Deleting Files and Folders

- Files and folders are moved to the recycle Bin when you select **Delete** from the file and folder menus in the File Explorer shown on page 99.

- Alternatively select **Remove** from the Drive website menu shown on page 100 to send files to the Bin (also sometimes known as the Trash).

- Then select **Yes** when asked if you are sure you want to move the file to the Bin.

- Open the Google Drive website as discussed on page 73 and select **Bin** from the left-hand panel to display all the files and folders you have moved to the Bin.

- Files and folders stay in the Bin until you empty it. To save Google Drive storage space, select **Bin** then **Empty bin** shown below.

- Alternatively right-click over a file or folder in the Bin and select **Restore** to move it back to its original location on all your computers or select **Delete forever** to remove it permanently from everywhere.

Windows PC

Managing Photos

As mentioned elsewhere, files such as photos can be uploaded to the Drive website by various methods, including dragging and dropping and cutting and pasting to the Drive folder in the File Explorer. Then they are uploaded to the Drive website. You can also use the **Upload** button in both the Drive and Photos websites, including uploading from external devices such as flash drives and SD cards.

| + Create   ↑ Upload |

Until recently photos were synced, i.e. mirrored, between the Drive and Photos websites. Google received feedback from users that this was confusing and in July 2019 stopped the syncing between Drive and Photos.

As discussed on page 93 and 108, a setting in the Google Photos app on Android and iOS devices allows you to select your Google Account as the destination for photos taken using your smartphone on tablet. These are then uploaded automatically, i.e. backed up, to your account in the Photos website at:

photos.google.com

- Clicking the 3-bar menu button shown on the right and near the bottom of page 102 displays a menu including an option to see who you have shared photos with.

- Clicking **Bin** on the same menu gives access to the recycle Bin discussed on page 101.

- **Settings** on the 3-bar menu includes options to buy more Google Drive storage or **Compress** photos from **Original** to **High quality (free unlimited storage)**.

- Clicking a photo on the Photos website opens the photo full-screen. A menu bar is displayed on the top right, as shown below.

- The 3-dot button shown on the right above displays options to **Download** the photo to your local storage such as a hard drive or flash drive. Also to display a **Slideshow** or **Rotate** an image.

- The dustbin icon above and on the right moves a photo to the recycle Bin discussed earlier.

- The star icon places a copy of the photo in your **Favourites Album**.

- The **Share** icon is used to send a copy of a photo in an e-mail to one of your contacts.

Creating a Link

- There is also an option to create a link to a photo on your Photos website. The link is copied and pasted into an e-mail. Anyone receiving the e-mail clicks the link to display the photo.

Create link

Android and iOS Tablets and Smartphones

Managing Files and Folders

Tablets and smartphones have limited local storage and, unlike PCs, don't have a Google Drive folder on the device itself. Instead these mobile computers have an app, as discussed on page 74, to enable you to view and manage files and folders on the Google Drive website.

- Open the app by tapping its icon shown on the right. The Drive website opens as shown below on an Android smartphone.

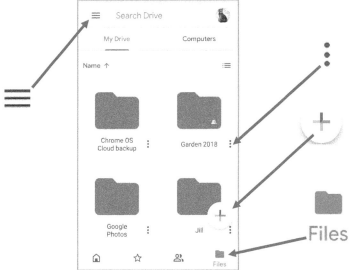

- Select **Files** shown above to view all your files and folders. Tap a folder to see files and sub-folders within the folder.

- Scroll down to view, in alphabetical order of file names, individual documents and photos which are not within folders.

- Tap the 3-dot menu button at the right of a file or folder as shown on page 104 to open a menu with options including **Remove** (to the Bin as discussed on page 101). The file menu includes options such as **Download**, **Rename**, **Make available offline**, **Open with** and **Copy link**, discussed shortly.

- Tap the ✛ icon at the lower right of the screen, shown on the right and on page 104, to open the **Create new** menu shown on page 78.

- Tap the 3-bar button shown on the right and on page 104 to open the menu shown below.

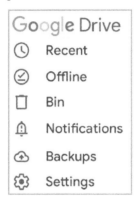

- Tap **Offline** to list files which have been saved on the . Internal Storage on your device

- **Bin** allows you to **Restore** files to their previous location or you can select **Delete forever**.

- **Settings > Backup and reset** is used to set or change the Google Account your files and folders are backed up to in Drive. (Also discussed on pages 92 and 93).

- **Settings > Clear cache** removes temporary copies of files and folders to save storage space.

Android and iOS Tablets and Smartphones

The Google Photos App

- Android and iOS tablets and smartphones have a dedicated Photos app, shown on the right, which can be downloaded and installed from the Play Store or App Store.

- The app can be used to upload and manage photos and videos on the website at **photos.google.com**.

- Photos and videos captured on a smartphone or tablet are backed up, i.e. uploaded automatically, to your Google Account on the Photos website.

- A tick in a cloud icon shown right is displayed when the backup is complete, as shown below on an Android smartphone.

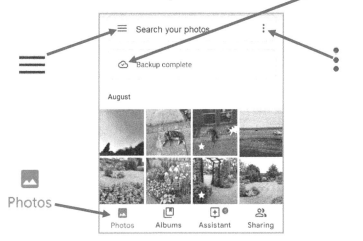

- Select **Photos** shown above to display all the images or tap **Albums** to display albums of photos and videos such as **Places**, **Favourites**, **Camera**, and **Download**.

- Tap the 3-button shown on the right and on page •
  106, to open a menu which includes the options •
  shown below.

- **Layout** shown above includes options to display
  photos on a **Day View**, **Month View** or a **Comfortable
  view** which displays single larger images.

- **Select** shown above lets you tick photos, as shown
  below, on which to carry out various tasks after
  tapping the icons higlighted in red and listed below.

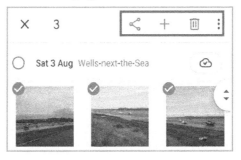

:   **Delete from device** or **Move to archive**. **(Archive** hides
:   photos from the **Photos** screen but keeps them in
     albums and folders).

Move to Bin as discussed on pages 101 and 108.

Create new Album, **Movie**, **Animation**, etc.

Share with e-mail contacts, Facebook, etc. Also
Create link, as discussed elsewhere in this book.

• Tapping anywhere on an unticked photo as shown on
page 106 displays the image enlarged on the screen
with the icons shown below, explained on page 103.

• Tapping the 3-dot menu button above displays
options to start a **Slideshow, Save to device, Add to
album, Print** and **Move to archive**.

• Tapping the 3-bar button shown on the right
and on page 106 displays options to display
photos in your **Device folders**, or in your
Archive or **Bin**, as shown on the left below.

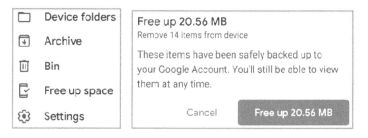

• **Free up space** shown on the left above is used to
remove photos and videos from your device that have
already been backed up, as shown on the right above.

• **Settings** shown above allows you to switch on **Back
up & sync**, as shown below, so that your photos and
videos are backed up to your Google Account in the
Photos website, as discussed in detail on page 93.

Upload, search, organise, edit & share your photos
from any device

Back up & sync

Google Chromebooks
Managing Files and Folders

- As discussed on page 35, Chromebooks are made by a number of manufacturers and are designed to work in the Cloud using the Chrome Web browser and the Chrome OS operating system.

- Chromebooks use the **My Drive** folder on the **Drive** website at: **drive.google.com**

- Files and folders are managed on the Internal Storage on the device in the Chromebook *Files App*, shown below.

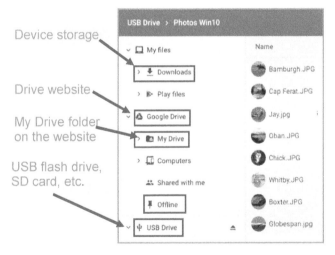

Device storage

Drive website

My Drive folder
on the website

USB flash drive,
SD card, etc.

- As shown above, a flash drive has been connected via one of the USB ports on the Chromebook. These ports enable various USB external devices to be connected as discussed in Chapter 13.

- Then files such as documents and photos can be uploaded to the Drive website by dragging and dropping using a mouse or two fingers on a touchpad.

- Files and folders can be *downloaded* to the **Downloads** folder, the limited Internal Storage on the Chromebook, or saved on an external device as discussed in Chapter 13, by dragging and dropping.

- A menu for the usual tools such as **Cut**, **Copy**, **Paste**, **Rename** and **Delete** can displayed by right-clicking a file or folder with a mouse or a two-finger press on a touchpad.

Managing Photos

As well as the Files App just described, Chromebooks use the Photos website at **photos.google.com** to upload and manage photos. The notes on pages 102 and 103 for the Windows PC also apply to the Chromebook.

photos.google.com   Create album, etc.   Upload

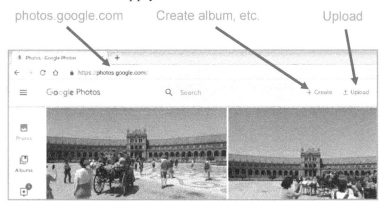

- Photos taken on a smartphone or tablet are automatically uploaded to the website. Photos taken using the camera on the Chromebook are saved in the Downloads folder.

- Deleted photos remain in the Bin for 60 days, unless the Bin is emptied or they are restored or permanently deleted.

9

Microsoft OneDrive

Introduction

OneDrive is Microsoft's Cloud Storage system and a rival to Google Drive and Dropbox discussed elsewhere in this book. The main purpose of OneDrive is to provide large amounts of cheap data storage on remote Web servers in the Cloud, to supplement the limited *local* storage on our own computers — desktops, laptops, tablets and smartphones. This is particularly necessary with the latest slimline, low memory Chromebook and Cloudbook laptops designed to take advantage of the Cloud.

OneDrive is pre-installed on Windows 10 computers and ready to use from starting up. As shown below, OneDrive can be used on all the major computing platforms in addition to Microsoft Windows. These include Android smartphones and tablets, Google Chromebooks, Apple Macs and Apple iOS devices (iPads and iPhones).

Windows 10   Android+Chromebook   iPad

This chapter covers OneDrive on Windows 10 computers. Much of the material is also relevant to Mac computers running the OneDrive app for Mac.

Chapter 10 discusses the use of OneDrive on Android and iOS tablets and smartphones as well as Chromebooks.

Accessibility

Any files you create on one computer in OneDrive are accessible on any other computer, anywhere. This includes tablets and smartphones as well as PCs, etc., on which the files may have been originally created. The only requirement to access the files is that you are connected to the Internet and signed into your Microsoft account.

Synchronization

As discussed in more detail shortly, OneDrive stores your files and folders in the *OneDrive folder* on the computer they are created on. When you save a file or folder on your device a copy is synced up to the *OneDrive website*. Depending on your settings, copies may be downloaded to the local storage on any other devices you sign into. Any changes, such as editing or deleting a file, will be mirrored on all of the other computers you are signed into.

Security

OneDrive automatically *backs up* copies of your files, i.e. documents, photos and videos, etc. These are stored on the Web servers in data centres around the world and securely managed by professionals. So should your computer break down, the copy on the Web server is still accessible from any computer, anywhere. However, if you *delete* a file or folder from the Web, it may be deleted from *every device*, *everywhere*, depending on your settings. It may be recoverable from the *Recycle Bin* for a limited time.

Therefore, for complete security, it's worth making extra backup copies of important files on *removable storage devices* such as flash drives or external disc drives, etc., as discussed in Chapter 13.

Installing Microsoft OneDrive

OneDrive was initially a Windows app but a version with similar features is available for Apple Macs. As discussed in Chapter 10, OneDrive files and folders can be accessed, managed and edited on Android and Apple (iOS) tablets and smartphones using the OneDrive App from the Play Store or App Store.

Windows 8, 8.1, 10 and 10 S

OneDrive is already built into later versions of Windows so it's ready to use straightaway — there's nothing to install. To use OneDrive you need a connection to the Internet and a Microsoft Account with a valid username and password.

Windows 7

Users of Windows 7 can use their Web browser such as Internet Explorer, Google Chrome or Firefox to download the app from the OneDrive website at:

onedrive.live.com

Select **Download**, as shown above.

- Select **Run** to launch **OneDriveSetup.exe**.

- After installation you will be asked to sign in with your Microsoft username and password.

- You will then be able to choose which files and folders are to be included in your OneDrive folder and synced between your other devices, as discussed shortly.

Payment Plans or Free Use of OneDrive

To view the various OneDrive options:

- Enter **onedrive.live.com** in the address bar in your Web browser such as Microsoft Edge, Firefox or Google Chrome and press **Return**.

- The OneDrive website opens as shown below.

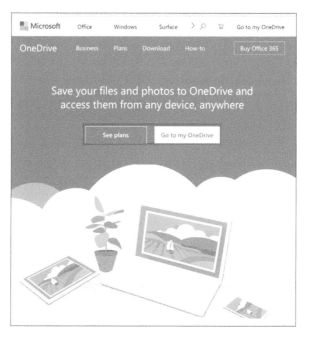

- Select **See plans** shown above and below to see the various free and payment options, as discussed on the next two pages. Most of the plans are based on the Office 365 software suite.

- Office 365 is available for all platforms including Windows PCs, Macs, Androids, Chromebooks, iPads and iPhones and includes online versions of Word, Excel and PowerPoint, etc., as well as OneDrive.

- Alternatively you can sign up for OneDrive *storage only* with **OneDrive Basic 5GB** for free or **OneDrive 100GB** for £1.99 per month.

- If you are using Microsoft Windows you will already be signed in with a Microsoft account and OneDrive will already be installed. However, you will still need to install Office 365, if required, as discussed below.

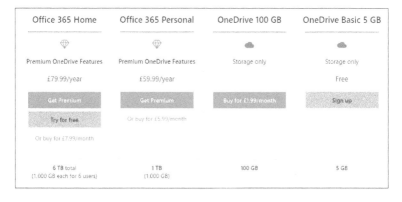

Office 365 Home	Office 365 Personal	OneDrive 100 GB	OneDrive Basic 5 GB
Premium OneDrive Features	Premium OneDrive Features	Storage only	Storage only
£79.99/year	£59.99/year		Free
Get Premium	Get Premium	Buy for £1.99/month	Sign up
Try for free	Or buy for £5.99/month		
Or buy for £7.99/month			
6 TB total (1,000 GB each for 6 users)	1 TB (1,000 GB)	100 GB	5 GB

- Select the plan you wish to use and either proceed to the **Checkout** to subscribe or click **Sign up** to use the **OneDrive Basic 5 GB**.

- **Office 365 Home** can be tried for free for one month.

- The above plans are discussed further on the next page.

- Once you have selected a plan and signed in you can go to your OneDrive website at:

onedrive.live.com

Microsoft Office 365

OneDrive when used on its own is free and gives *5GB* of cloud storage. It can also be used as part of the Microsoft Office 365 software suite. Apart from OneDrive, this includes *online* or *Web-based* versions of popular programs such as Microsoft Word, Excel and PowerPoint, etc., discussed in Chapter 12.

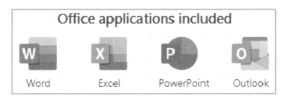

The current payment plans are shown below. These all give *1TB* of Cloud storage space *per user*.

Home Users

- The most popular plan is Office 365 Personal, costing £59.99 per year or £5.99 per month. This can be used by one person across PCs, Macs, Androids, iPads, etc.

- Office 365 Home (£79.99 per year or £7.99 a month) allows up to 6 people to use the suite on all their devices.

- Office Home & Student 2019 allows Classic Office apps (Word, Excel, PowerPoint) to be installed on one PC or Mac for a one-time purchase price of £119.99.

Business and Education

- Separate schemes are available for business and education users. Educators and students are eligible for Office 365 Education for free. A valid school email address must be provided.

Starting to Use OneDrive

Windows 10 and 10 S

As stated earlier, OneDrive is built into later versions of the Windows operating system, so there's nothing to install. It's already present on the Start Menu as shown below on the left, opened by clicking the Windows icon shown on the right.

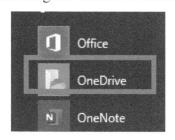

OneDrive should already be pinned as a tile on the Windows Start Screen, as shown on the right above. If not, right-click on **OneDrive** shown on the left above, then click **Pin to Start** shown below.

If not already present, an icon for the OneDrive folder can be placed on the Taskbar at the bottom of the screen by clicking **More** and **Pin to taskbar** as shown above.

The OneDrive Taskbar Icon in Windows 10

An icon for OneDrive, shown on the left, should appear on the Notification Area of the Taskbar at the bottom right of the screen, as shown below.

- If the OneDrive icon is not shown, it might need to be displayed by clicking the **Show hidden icons** button shown on the right.

- *Double-clicking* the OneDrive icon, shown again on the right, opens the OneDrive folder discussed on page 119.

- A *single click* of the OneDrive icon opens the window shown below. Click **More** to display the menu shown on the right below. Alternatively, simply *right-click* the OneDrive icon to display the menu.

Where are OneDrive Files and Folders?

Your OneDrive files and folders exist in two places:

- The OneDrive *folder* on the Internal Storage of your computer such as a hard drive, SSD or eMMC, discussed in Chapter 13.

- The OneDrive *website*, discussed on page 125.

- If you have limited local storage you may choose not to keep all of your OneDrive files on your computer.

The OneDrive Folder

This is used to store your files consisting of documents, photos and videos. Files and folders within the OneDrive folder are viewed and managed in the Windows 10 File Explorer, as shown below.

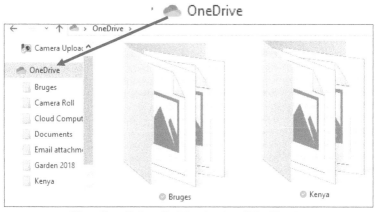

The OneDrive Folder in the File Explorer

As well as the easily accessible icon and **OneDrive** name in the File Explorer shown above, the OneDrive folder can also be viewed in its precise location on the hard disc/SSD at: **C: > Users > Your name > OneDrive**

Opening the OneDrive Folder

There are several alternative ways to quickly open the OneDrive folder:

1. Open the File Explorer by clicking its icon on the Taskbar at the bottom of the screen, as shown on the right. Click on **OneDrive** in the left-hand panel as shown on page 119.

2. Click the OneDrive icon shown on the right and on the Taskbar at the bottom of the screen, as shown at the bottom of page 117.

3. *Double-click* the OneDrive icon, shown on the right, in the Notification Area on the right of the Taskbar at the bottom of the screen, as shown near the top of page 118.

4. *Right-click* the OneDrive icon shown again on the right and on page 118. Then select **Open folder** as shown at the bottom of page 118.

5. Open the File Explorer as discussed at the top of this page and scroll down the left-hand panel and select:

   This PC > OS(C:) > Users >Your name > OneDrive

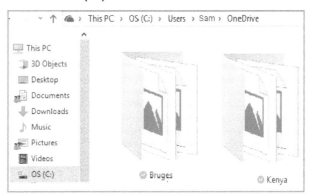

Saving Files and Folders in OneDrive

Save As:

- Use the **File/Save As** option to save a document when using a program such as MS Word, Publisher or Excel. Select the OneDrive folder in the File Explorer, as shown on page 119.

- Alternatively create some sub-folders in the OneDrive folder as discussed on page 122. Then select one of these and use **Save As**.

Drag and Drop

- Select an existing file or folder in the File Explorer then, holding down the left mouse button, drag it to the OneDrive folder and release the button.

Cut and Paste or Copy and Paste

- *Right-click* over a file or folder in the File Explorer then select **Cut** or **Copy** then right-click over the OneDrive folder and select **Paste**. (**Cut** removes the file or folder from its original location, **Copy** doesn't).

Automatic Backing Up and Downloading

- As discussed shortly, selected files and folders can be automatically backed up to the OneDrive Website.

- You can also specify which files and folders are automatically synced down to the local storage on the computer you are currently working on.

- Th OneDrive website also has an option to select and *upload* individual files and folders.

- Selected files and folders can also be *downloaded* from the OneDrive website. E.g. to work on a file *offline* or to download a file to removable storage, such as a flash drive, to give a copy to someone else.

Creating Folders in OneDrive

- Open the File Explorer by clicking its icon on the Taskbar, as shown on the right.

- Select the folder in which the new folder is to be created, such as **OneDrive > Camera Roll** shown below.

- Select **New folder** shown on the right and below, enter a name for the folder, such as **Snaps** and press **Return**.

New folder

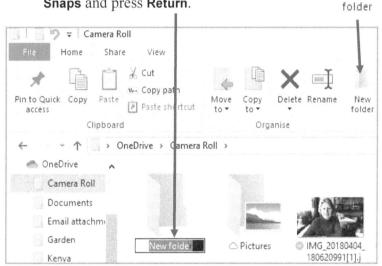

- The quick access path to the new folder in the left-hand panel of the File Explorer is then:

OneDrive > Camera Roll > Snaps

- The actual location of the folder on the hard drive is:

This PC > OS (C:) > Users > Jim > OneDrive > Camera Roll > Snaps

- You can also create a hierarchy of *sub-folders* within the OneDrive folder.

Choosing which Folders to Download

- As discussed earlier, files you save to OneDrive are automatically synced to the OneDrive website on a remote Web server computer. From there they are accessible to any online computer you are signed into.

- OneDrive allows you to select which folders are to be downloaded and saved on a particular computer. (Assuming you have enough storage on the device).

- Click the OneDrive Taskbar icon shown on the right and then select **More** and **Settings** shown on page 118.

- Select the **Account** tab and then **Choose folders** as shown below.

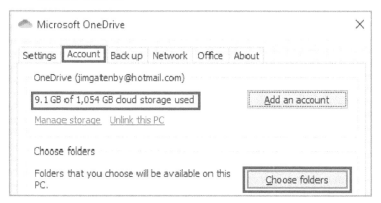

- Select the OneDrive folders you wish to be synced down from the Web to your computer, or select **Make all files available**, as shown on the next page. As shown above, the amount of storage you have in the Cloud (**9.1GB**) is displayed. Downloading all of this would use up valuable space on some computers with limited Internal Storage.

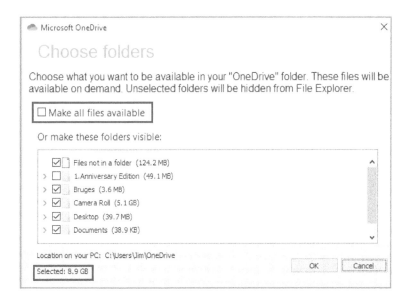

- The above settings only apply to the computer on which you are currently working.

- The above window also shows the amount of data, **8.9GB** in this example, which will be downloaded from the OneDrive website to the storage on your computer's hard drive, SSD, etc. This should be taken into consideration if your computer has very limited storage space remaining.

- If you remove a tick from one of the folders as shown above, the folder will be removed from your computer. The folder will still be available online, i.e. on the OneDrive website.

- **Files on Demand**, as shown on page 131, allows you to make files generally only available online, to save storage space on your computer. Selected files can be downloaded and viewed as required.

The OneDrive Website

- The OneDrive Website contains all of your OneDrive files and folders. As just discussed, depending on your settings, some or all of these may also be saved on the local storage of a particular computer.

- Instead of the File Explorer, the OneDrive files and folders are viewed in your Web browser, such as Microsoft Edge, Google Chrome or Firefox, etc.

- Files you save in your OneDrive folder discussed on page 119 and 120 are automatically synced, i.e. copied, to the OneDrive website.

Viewing the OneDrive Website

- To view the OneDrive files and folders stored online, on a Web server, *right-click* over **OneDrive** shown in the File Explorer on the right, then select **View online** from the menu shown below.

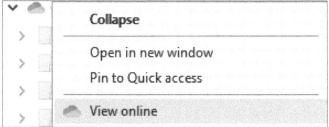

- The OneDrive website opens as shown on page 126.

- Alternatively, to open the website, right-click the OneDrive Taskbar icon and select **View online** as shown on page 118.

After selecting **View online** shown at the bottom of the previous page, the OneDrive website is displayed, as shown below. This shows all of your OneDrive files and folders, some or all of which will also be stored on your computer.

Folders on the OneDrive Website

You can also right-click over individual files and folders in the File Explorer and select **View online** to see the copies of the same files and folders on the Web server.

Uploading Files and Folders to the OneDrive Website

- Select the folder on the OneDrive website into which the files or folders are to be uploaded.

- Select **Upload** shown on the OneDrive website above then select **Files** or **Folder**.

- The File Explorer opens, enabling you to locate and select the file or folder you wish to upload to the OneDrive website.

- The file or folder to be uploaded may be on your local hard drive/SSD or on an external plug-in device such as a flash drive, as discussed in Chapter 13.

- Select **Open** and the file or folder will be uploaded to the OneDrive website and accessible to any Internet computer you are signed into.

Backing Up Files and Folders to OneDrive

- Normally when you are working on a document such as a report or spreadsheet, etc., you will probably use **Save As** from the **File menu** to place the file in a folder of your choice within OneDrive.

- However, if you don't specify a OneDrive folder, your files are still backed up automatically.

- Settings in Windows 10 allow all your important files and folders to be saved *by default* on the OneDrive website where they can be accessed by any computer.

The Default Backup Location

- Click the OneDrive icon on the Notification Area of the Taskbar to open the window shown at the bottom of page 118.

- Select **More**, **Settings** and **Backup** as shown below.

- Under **Important PC Folders** shown below, select **Manage backup** to open the window shown on page 128.

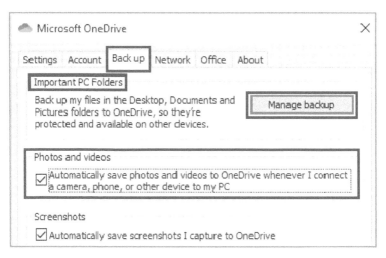

- If any folders need backing up, select **Start backup**, which appears when necessary, at the bottom of the window shown below.

- If you create, say, a Word document and don't select a folder in the File Explorer, the file is saved by default on the local storage **(C:)** of your computer at:

OS (C:) › Users › Jim › OneDrive › Camera Roll › Pictures › Documents ›

- The file (**Testing Default Save location.docx** in this example) is also automatically uploaded and saved on the OneDrive website at:

Files > Camera Roll > Pictures > Documents

- View the OneDrive upload process by clicking the Taskbar icon shown on the right.

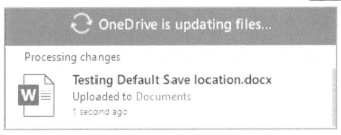

Backing Up Photos and Videos to OneDrive

- Tick the box shown below and on page 127 to automatically save photos and videos to OneDrive.

- In the example below, an SD card containing photos and a video was placed in the SD card slot on a PC. The automatic uploading process of saving photos and a video was shown in the OneDrive window opened from the Taskbar icon as discussed on page 118, as shown in the extract below displaying the video.

The photos were saved on the **(C:)** drive on the PC as shown below in **OS(C:) > Users > Jim > OneDrive** ......, etc.

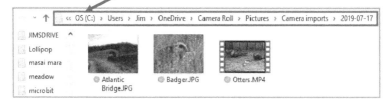

To save clicking through all the sub-folders shown above, the files can be accessed more easily in the File Explorer at:

› This PC › Pictures › Camera imports › 2019-07-17

- The photos and the video also appear in the OneDrive website at:

Camera Roll > Pictures > Camera imports > 2019-07-19

Recycle bin

- Viewing the OneDrive website is discussed on pages 125 and 126.

Managing OneDrive Storage

As discussed earlier, all your files (and folders) exist on the OneDrive website, accessible to any computer anywhere. Depending on the settings on an individual computer, OneDrive files may are also be kept on the local storage such as a hard drive or SSD. Some potential problems are:

Deleting Files

- If you delete an *Online-only* file (or folder), it is deleted from everywhere and is not sent to the **Recycle bin** on the OneDrive website, outlined in red above, unlike files deleted from local storage.

- When a file which has been saved both online and locally is deleted, it is removed from both online and local storage.

- Deleted local files can be recovered for up to 30 days from the OneDrive **Recycle bin** in the left-hand panel of the website, as shown outlined in red on page 130.

- If you have irreplaceable family or other photos or important documents, for safety these should be backed up in a separate folder **outside of OneDrive**. They will then be safe from any mass OneDrive accidental deleting operations.

- It's also a good idea to back up important data on *removable storage* such as a flash drive or external hard drive, as discussed in Chapter 13.

- Computers designed for the Cloud such as Chromebooks and Cloudbooks and also tablets and smartphones may only have 16-64GB of on-device storage. So online storage is essential.

- If you need to use your computer *offline*, where there is no Internet, then some storage on the device itself is essential. *Files on Demand* is a new feature in OneDrive designed to give you access to your files while saving space on your hard drive, etc.

Files on Demand

This a new feature on Windows 10 and Mac computers.

- When this is switched on as discussed shortly, all your OneDrive files become *online-only* and are marked in the File Explorer with an empty Cloud *status icon*.

- Online-only files are listed in the File Explorer but are not taking up disc space.

- When you click an online-only file in the File Explorer, it is downloaded and saved on the local device storage. It can now be viewed anytime with or without an Internet connection.

- This *locally available* file is marked with the icon shown on the right and below.

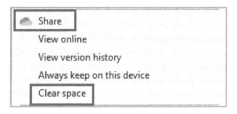

- To change a file back to online-only and free-up space on your hard drive, etc., right-click the file in the File Explorer and select **Clear space** from the menu, as shown below.

- Locally available files may be *automatically deleted* if storage space on the device becomes very low.

- To keep a file permanently on your hard drive, etc., right-click the file in the File Explorer and select **Always keep on this device**, as shown above and ticked below.

- The file is now **Always available on this device**, both with and without an Internet connection. It is denoted by the green circle and white tick shown here.

Switching On Files on Demand

- Click the OneDrive icon shown on the right, and on the Taskbar on page 118.

- Select **More** and **Settings** as shown on page 118 then click the **Settings** tab shown below.

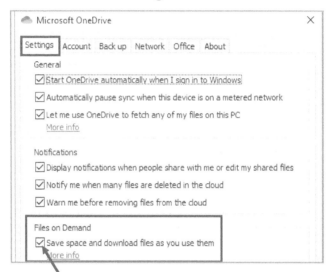

- Click to tick the check box if you want to switch on **Files on Demand** shown above, then click **OK**.

- Check boxes above switch on notifications when many files are deleted from the Cloud. Also to warn you before removing files from the Cloud.

- The status icons for the same files and folders can be different on different computers, depending on whether **Files on Demand** or **Always keep on this device** is ticked on those particular computers.

Online-only   Locally available   Always available

Sending a OneDrive Link

This can be used to send an Internet link to allow friends or colleagues to access your documents or photos, etc. In this example, a link to a folder containing 44 photos of the city of Seville was sent, as follows:

- Right-click the file or folder in the Windows File Explorer to display the menu shown on page 132. Click **Share**.
- Enter the name or email address of each recipient and press **Enter** or **Return** after each.

- Click **Anyone with the link can edit** shown above left to open the **Link settings** shown above on the right.
- **Set expiry date** on the right above limits the time when the link will still be available. **Set password** requires you to provide recipients with a password.

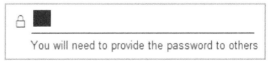

- Click **Apply** shown above right then click **Send**. On receiving the email your contact(s) click **Open** to view the files or folders accessed by the link you've sent.

10

OneDrive on Mobile Devices

Introduction

The last chapter discussed the use of OneDrive within its original environment, the Microsoft Windows operating system. OneDrive apps have also been developed for the main mobile computer operating systems such as Android and iOS (iPads and iPhones). Also ChromeOS, used in the range of slimline Chromebooks designed for the Cloud.

World leading MS Office software such as Word and Excel can be downloaded free for Android, Chrome OS and iOS mobile devices. Or you can subscribe to one of the Office 365 plans discussed on pages 114-116, which include these apps as well as the OneDrive mobile app and *1TB (Terabyte)* of storage. (Compared with only *5GB* if you are using the free, storage-only version of OneDrive.)

Nowadays many people use more than one computer - such as a desktop, laptop, tablet and smartphone. These may be used in several different locations - at home, at work, in school or college, on a train or in a café, etc.

OneDrive, together with the mobile Microsoft apps such as Word and Excel, makes it feasible to continue working on documents or looking at photos and videos in different places, wherever there is an Internet connection.

While creating and editing documents on the move is easier on a laptop or tablet computer, a smartphone can be used to view photos and videos stored on your OneDrive. Also to read and check documents, perhaps to find information when away from the home or office, etc.

OneDrive Across Platforms

- This book was mainly written on a desktop Windows 10 PC using Microsoft Publisher, saving files in the **.pub** file format shown below.

- Each chapter was saved as a file in a folder called **Chapters** within a folder called **Cloud Computing**, which is itself a sub-folder of the **OneDrive** folder.

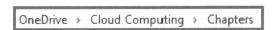

- The work was done in OneDrive in a number of locations, apart from my desktop PC, using MS Publisher on Windows laptop computers.

- Files were also saved in the universally acceptable **.pdf** format, shown below, allowing them to be reviewed anywhere, on my Android, Chromebook and iPad mobile devices. (The MS Publisher **.pub** file format is not currently compatible with Android and iOS smartphones and tablets).

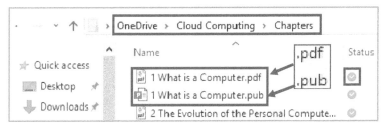

- In the example above, all the files have the **Always available** green status icon shown on the right, as discussed in Chapter 9, i.e. they are saved *online* and on the *local hard drive*, etc.

- Examples of the use of OneDrive across different devices are shown on the next page.

Documents

Shown below is page 117 of this book, created in Microsoft Publisher on a Windows PC and saved in OneDrive as a PDF file. Then it could be viewed on any computer such as the iPad shown on the right and, if necessary, the Chromebook and Android at the bottom of the page.

Windows 10 PC

Apple iPad

Photos and Videos

The photo below was taken in Kenya on a DSLR camera and imported to OneDrive from the camera's SD card. SD cards are discussed on page 129 and in Chapter 13.

Acer Chromebook

Android Smartphone

Installing OneDrive on Mobile Devices

- OneDrive is available free as an app from the Google Play Store for Androids and Chromebooks and from the App Store for iOS devices (iPads and iPhones).

- The following method of installing the app on Androids and Chromebooks is very similar to that used on iOS devices.

- Search for OneDrive in your app store, then tap or click **INSTALL** or the download icon, as shown below.

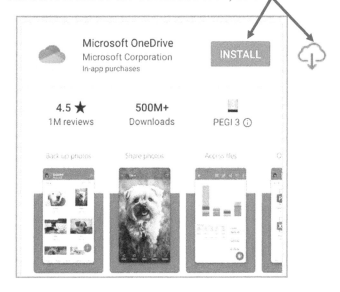

- The OneDrive app is downloaded and installed on your device. Now tap or click **OPEN**, as shown below.

- The **Welcome** screen opens as shown below. Swipe left to display more screens displaying some of the features of OneDrive.

- If you already have a Microsoft account, tap or click **Sign in** shown above and enter your e-mail address and password.

- Alternatively select **No account? Create one!** shown above. You need to enter an e-mail address or phone number, a password and your date of birth.

- After signing in, you are presented with details of Office 365, as shown on the next page.

- If you've created a new account you are presented with the details of **Office 365 Personal**, as shown below and discussed in Chapter 9.
- Tap or click **GET PREMIUM** to subscribe to Office 365 Personal.
- If you have previously subscribed to Office 365 Personal tap or click **GOT IT** which appears instead of **GET PREMIUM — FIRST MONTH FREE**, as shown in green near the bottom of this page. This completes the installation of OneDrive if you are already a subscriber to Office 365.

- If you don't wish to start subscribing to Office 365 Personal click the **X** at the top of the window, next to **Get Premium** shown on page 140.

- You are then asked **Is OneDrive Basic enough?** and reminded of the extra storage (1TB) which comes with a subscription to Office 365.

- You can then select either GO BACK for another chance to subscribe to Office 365 or STAY BASIC to go with the free OneDrive plan with 5GB of storage.

Is OneDrive Basic enough?

Office 365 comes with enhanced OneDrive features and much more storage (1 TB!).

GO BACK   STAY BASIC

Start Camera Upload

- At the end of the OneDrive set up process there is an option to **Start Camera Upload**. This means the photos and videos taken on your device can be uploaded over Wi-Fi and will be available on all your other computers and on the **OneDrive.com** website.

Your memories, everywhere

Turn on camera upload and every snap you take on this phone will be available on your PC, tablet and OneDrive.com

Start Camera Upload

Not now

Photos and videos will only be uploaded over Wi-Fi.
Change this setting

Launching OneDrive

At the end of the installation process, an icon is placed on your apps screen. Or you may prefer to drag it to your Home Screen or to the Favourites Tray or Dock at the bottom of the screen, as shown below.

OneDrive

- Tap the app shown above left to launch OneDrive.
- If you've created a new OneDrive account, new empty folders labelled **Attachments**, **Documents**, **Pictures** are provided, as shown below.

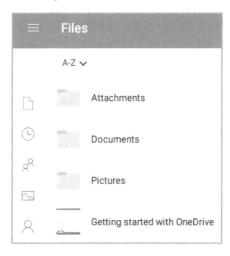

- Tap **Getting started with OneDrive** shown above to view a comprehensive introduction to OneDrive.

- If you've signed in with a OneDrive account used on other computers, your existing files and folders should appear in the newly installed OneDrive app, as shown below on an Android smartphone.

- iOS devices (iPads and iPhones) have broadly similar features to those described on the next few pages, accessed by 3-dot menus like those shown below.

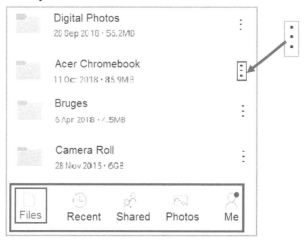

- **Files** shown above displays all your files and folders.

- **Recent** shows the MS Office documents opened recently.

- **Shared** lists the files and photos you have shared with other people.

- **Photos** above displays thumbnails of all your photos in chronological order.

- **Me** opens the menu shown on page 146.

- On Chromebooks the buttons for the above options, **Files**, **Recent**, etc., may appear in a vertical list near the top left of the screen.

- Tap the 3-button menu shown to the right of a file or folder to open a menu as shown below.

- Similar options can be displayed across the top of the screen on Androids and Chromebooks by tapping and *holding* a file or folder, as shown below.

- **Share** sends a link to your OneDrive file or folder via e-mail to allow someone else to view and perhaps edit a document or folder, as discussed on page 134.

- To move a file, tap **Move** shown above, select the file or folder to be moved then select the destination folder and tap **MOVE HERE**.

- The **Save** option shown above and to the right is used to download a copy of a file to the **Downloads** folder within the Android **Files** app *on your device*.

- Tap **Save** on the menu shown above, then tap **SAVE** again as shown below to start the download.

- Tap the Android **Files** icon on your app screen shown on the right to display the **Downloads** folder shown below.

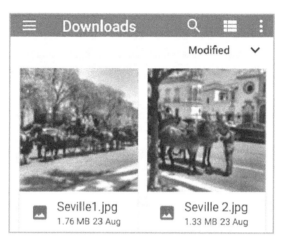

- Tap and hold a file in the **Downloads** folder to display a menu including options to copy, move and delete the file. Also to compress the file to save device storage.

- Tap or click **Delete** shown on the menu on page 144 to move a file or folder to the OneDrive recycle bin discussed on pages 130 and 131.

- **Keep offline** shown on page 144, saves a copy of a file or folder on your device so you can read it offline (as well as online). An offline file or folder is marked in OneDrive with the icon shown on the right and below.

- To switch between *offline* use and *online-only* use, tap and hold a file or folder then tap one of the two icons below which alternate on the menu below.

The One Drive Me Menu

- Tap the **Me** button shown below and on page 143 to open the menu shown below. On iOS devices the **Me** button is at the top left of the screen.

- **Files Available Offline** above lists the files you can use where there is no Internet connection.

- **Recycle Bin** is discussed on pages 130 and 131.

- **Notifications** lists albums created by OneDrive and other OneDrive tasks such as enhancing a photo.

- **Settings** includes the option **Clear space on your device** to delete photos you have already backed up.

- There is also an option to switch **Camera upload** on or off (as discussed on page 141).

Dropbox Cloud Storage

Introduction

Dropbox, Inc is a major American Cloud storage company, founded in 2007 and now having hundreds of millions of users worldwide. Versions of the Dropbox app are available for all types of computer - desktops, laptops, tablets and smartphones, for individual and business users.

Dropbox has similar features and functions to the other major Cloud storage systems such as Google Drive and Microsoft OneDrive discussed earlier. These include:

- Some storage space in the Cloud provided free, with more available on various subscription plans.

- *Uploading* files to the **dropbox.com** website so they can be accessed anywhere, on any computer.

- *Synchronisation* to apply changes to a file made on one computer to all your devices. *Selective synchronisation* to save space on your hard drive, etc., by keeping infrequently used files *online only*.

- Sending *links* to friends, family, etc., enabling them to view and perhaps edit documents and photos.

- Automatically backing up photos to the Dropbox website from a phone, SD card, flash drive, etc.

- Compatibility with online, i.e. Web-based versions, of major apps, such as MS Word, Excel, PowerPoint and Google Docs, Sheets and Slides.

- *Recovering* accidentally deleted files and previous versions of files for up to 30 days.

Cloud Storage

- The 2GB of Dropbox Cloud free storage for your files is small compared with other Cloud storage systems. OneDrive provides 5GB and Google Drive gives a more useful 15GB of free storage.

- One of the main purposes of Cloud computing is to provide extra storage for your files. The 2GB of Dropbox free Cloud storage is eclipsed by relatively inexpensive local flash drives and SD cards, with capacities ranging from 16GB to 256GB.

- It's very easy to fill 2GB of storage, especially if you're saving a lot of photos and videos. If you use up all your free storage, Dropbox stops working and will not upload files to the Cloud.

- However, deleting some files and folders should start Dropbox working again.

- To provide more useful amounts of Cloud storage, Dropbox offers several payment plans, billed monthly or yearly, as shown below for individual users.

Basic	Plus	Professional
Free	£7.99 / month	£16.58 / month
Your current plan	Get started	Get started
2GB	2TB (2,048GB)	3TB (3,072GB)

- Separate plans are available for business users including options offering as much space as you need.

- Free 30-day trials are available for Dropbox Professional and Dropbox Business users.

Web-based Apps

As discussed elsewhere in this book, running apps in the Cloud has some important advantages over locally-based programs. These include the following:

- Apps are executed in a Web server, which you can access through any of the popular Web browsers.

- The apps on the Web server are kept up-to-date by professionals - no need to keep updating your device.

MS Office Online and Google Docs, Sheets and Slides

Dropbox can use the Microsoft and Google apps shown below, after you select **Create** on the Dropbox website.

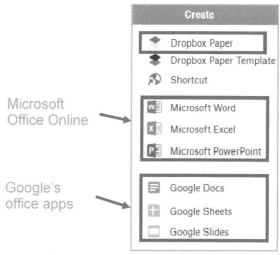

Dropbox Paper

Dropbox Paper, shown at the top above, is an app for producing text documents such as tables, to-do-lists and timelines used for planning projects and collaborating with others in a team. All types of media such as photos and videos can be inserted from a variety of sources.

Installing Dropbox

Windows PCs

- Open the website **www.dropbox.com** and click **Download the app** to download the installer progam **DropboxInstaller.exe**.

- Click **Run** to install the Dropbox app.

- Enter your e-mail address and password and click **Sign in**.

- Click **Open my Dropbox** then click **Get Started**.

- Click **Next** three times to learn about Dropbox and its plans such as Dropbox Basic and Plus. Choose between syncing **local files** and **online-only** files.

- Dropbox appears as a folder in the left-hand panel of the Windows File Explorer as shown below.

- To save files and folders in Dropbox, drag and drop their icons onto the **Dropbox** folder shown on the right and on the left of the File Explorer.

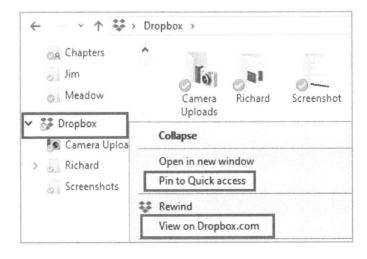

- Right-click **Dropbox** shown in the File Explorer on the previous page to open the menu shown under the word **Collapse**.

- Click **Pin to Quick access** to place a copy of the Dropbox name and icon under **Quick access** at the top of the File Explorer left-hand panel.

- The Dropbox folder is actually stored on your hard drive **(C:)** at the location shown below in **Users**:

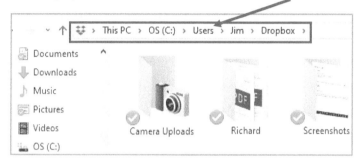

- Any files you save in the Dropbox folder will be synced up to the website at **www.dropbox.com** and accessible to any other computers you are signed into with your Dropbox account.

- Right-click over **Dropbox** (or any of its sub-folders and files) shown on page 150. Then Select **View on Dropbox.com** shown on the menu on page 150 to open the file or folder on the Dropbox website, shown on page 158.

- The circular icons as shown above, next to a file or folder, indicate the sync status as follows:

Sync complete   Sync in progress   Not syncing

Using the Dropbox App
Windows PCs

- Click the Dropbox icon on the Notification Area of the Taskbar at the bottom right of the screen, as shown on the right and below.

- The sync progress monitoring window pops up as shown in part below. The functions of the icons at the top right of the window are listed below.

 Create new item in Microsoft Word, Google Docs, etc., as discussed on page 149.

 Open Dropbox Paper app, mentioned on page 149.

 Open dropbox.com website, discussed on page 158.

 Open Dropbox folder, discussed on page 150.

 Access and manage your Dropbox settings. (Your own initials will appear in the blue circle.)

Selective Sync

Windows PCs

Files that you drag and drop or **Save** to your Dropbox folder are saved on your hard drive and also synced up to your Dropbox account on the Web.

Selective Sync allows you to to save space on your hard drive by removing files which you don't use very often. Online copies are still available in your Dropbox account.

- Click the Dropbox icon shown on the top right of page 152, then click the blue button shown on the right and on page 152 to open the settings menu. Click **Preferences...** from the menu.

- From the **Dropbox Preferences** menu which opens, click **Sync** shown on the right.

- Click **Selective Sync...** as shown below.

- Remove the ticks from folders you don't want to keep on your hard drive and click **Update**. They will still be accessible in your Dropbox online Web account.

Managing Files and Folders

Windows PCs

Deleting a File or Folder

- Drag a file or folder in the File Explorer and drop it in the Recycle Bin as shown on page 91.

- Alternatively right-click over the file or folder in the Dropbox folder (or click the 3-dot elipsis menu button on the website, as shown on pages 158). Select **Delete** from the menu to move the file or folder to the **Recycle Bin** or to start using Selective Sync.

- Select **Yes** and then **Delete everywhere** or select **See sync options** as discussed on page 153 if you just want to save space on your hard drive.

Restoring a File or Folder

- Select the Recycle Bin on the left of the File Explorer and right-click over a file or folder then select **Restore** from the menu.

- Alternatively open the Dropbox website and select **Files** then **Deleted files**, as shown on page 158.

- Click the box on the left to tick the files and folders to be restored, as shown below, then click **Restore**, followed by **Restore** again or **Restore all files**.

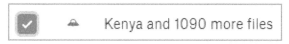
Kenya and 1090 more files

- There is also an option, shown below, to **Permanently delete** files so they cannot be restored.

Installing Dropbox
Android and iOS

The Dropbox app can be downloaded and installed from the Play Store for Androids and Chromebooks and the App Store for iOS devices (iPads and iPhones).

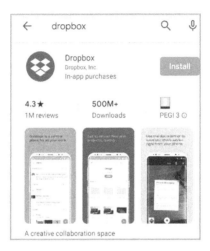

- Tap **Install** to download the app and then after a short time tap **Open**.

- **SIGN IN** with an existing Dropbox e-mail address and password or tap **SIGN UP FOR DROPBOX**.

- Choose your plan, either Dropbox Plus or stay with Dropbox Basic as shown on page 148.

Starting to Use Dropbox

Android and iOS

Tap the Dropbox icon shown on the right on your apps screen to display the Dropbox **Home** screen shown below.

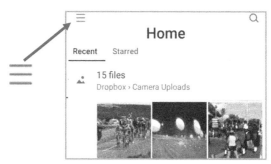

- Tap the 3-bar menu shown above to display the menu shown on the left below, including options to display **Files**, **Photos**, files available **Offline** and **Settings**.

- Tap the + icon at the bottom right of the screen, shown right, to display the **Add to Dropbox** menu shown on the right below.

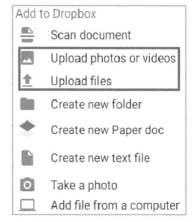

Managing Files and Folders
Android and iOS

- Select a file or folder in **Files**, shown in the left-hand menu on page 156, such as **Cats** shown below.

- Tap the tick shown above and right to switch on file selection as shown below with a white tick in a blue background. Tap the double tick shown right and below to select all files and folders.

- Selected files and folders can now be downloaded to your device by tapping the icon shown on the right and below.

- Tap the 3-dot menu button shown below to view the menu shown on the right below, showing options to apply to selected files.

Save to Device
Copy
Move
Delete

Save to Device above is greyed out when *folders* are selected.

- Tap the 3-dot button below a file or folder, to display a menu with further options to apply to individual files and folders, such as **Share**, **Copy**, **Rename**, **Move** and **Delete**.

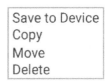

The Dropbox Website

Files and folders are accessible via the Dropbox folder in the File Explorer in PCs and via the Dropbox app in mobile devices. They can also be accessed in a Web browser on the **dropbox.com** website on all types of computing device.

Shown below is the left-hand side of the **dropbox.com** website open in the Microsoft Edge browser.

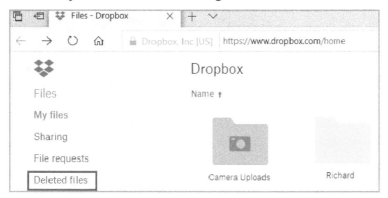

- **Deleted files** shown above allows deleted files in the Recycle Bin to be restored to their original locations, as discussed on page 154. On the right of the Dropbox Web page is an ellipsis or 3-dot menu button as shown on the right. Tap the button to display several options, including those shown below on the right.

- The **Upload** options allow you to browse your hard drive, etc., and devices such as SD cards and flash drives (discussed in Chapter 13) for files such as photos to upload to the website.

Importing Photos and Videos

Windows PCs

- Select **Preferences...** on the menu as discussed on page 153, then select **Import** on the **Dropbox Preferences** menu.

- Under **Camera Upload** select either **Photos only** or **Photos and videos**.

- Select **Change AutoPlay Settings**, then select either **Use AutoPlay for all media and devices** or select **Choose what to do do with each type of media** as shown below.

Choose what happens when you insert each type of media or device

☑ Use AutoPlay for all media and devices

Removable drives

⊟ Removable drive   Import photos and videos (Dropbox)

☐ Choose what to do with each type of media

- When you insert a removable device such as a flash drive containing photos, the **Camera Upload** window appears as shown below:

Keep your memories safe

All your photos and videos will be automatically saved to Dropbox

☐ **Include videos** for all devices you plug in.

Don't ask again   Start import   Cancel

- Click **Start Import** to find the photos and videos and upload them to the Dropbox **Camera Uploads** folder.

Importing Photos and Videos
Android, iOS and Chromebooks

- Tap the 3-bar menu screen shown on the Home ☰ screen on the right to display the menu shown on ☰ the left on page 156.

- Scroll down and select **Settings**. Scroll down the next menu and switch **Camera uploads** and **Upload video** On, if necessary, as shown below.

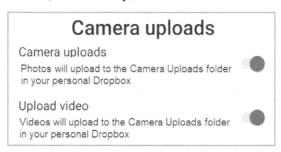

Sharing a Link

Copy link

All Devices

The general method is the same on all types of computer.

- Open the Dropbox folder, then right-click the file or folder or tap the 3-dot menu button next to a file or folder.

- Select **Copy Dropbox link** or **Copy link**.

- The link is copied to your *clipboard* and can then be pasted into an e-mail to your contacts.

- The recipient can tap or click the link in the e-mail to view, download and perhaps edit the document or photo, etc. (Links are also discussed on page 134).

12
Web-based Apps

Introduction

For many years it was normal for *apps*, (originally known as *application software* or *programs*), to be saved on the hard disc drive inside of a desktop or laptop computer. Software packages were bought on "floppy" magnetic discs and later CDs and DVDs. The software had be copied from the CD, etc., onto the hard drive.

Essential and very widely used software such as Microsoft Office, (Word and Excel, etc.,) cost several hundred pounds for installation on a single computer.

Laptops and desktop computers with software and data files stored locally on their hard disc are still widely used, although apps are nowadays downloaded from the Internet. However, recent years have seen an explosion in the use of tablets, smartphones, Chromebooks and Cloudbooks. Apart from leisure activities, these mobile devices are being used for serious computing work, such as to access files on the move, away from a desktop computer.

These mobile devices do not have the space for large hard drives on which to store bulky software such as Microsoft Office. However, mobile devices can compensate for this by using *Web-based apps* and Cloud Storage on Web server computers in *data centres*, as discussed earlier in this book. Even large desktop and laptop computers with high capacity hard drives and SSD on-board storage can benefit from the use of Web-based apps and Cloud Storage, as discussed on the next page.

Advantages of Web-based Apps

Web-based apps are computer programs running *Online* in a remote *Web server* computer. They are accessed using a *Web browser* running on your own (*client*) computer. Some advantages compared with locally-based apps are:

- The Web-based apps are managed by professionals in a data centre and should be secure and up-to-date. You don't need to install new versions on all your computers as you do with locally-based apps.

- Web-based apps are compatible with all the popular Web browsers such as Chrome, Firefox, Internet Explorer, Edge, etc. New versions of locally-based apps may not be compatible with your computer.

- Web-based apps are not saved on your computer and so do not use up storage space. This is particularly important with tablets, smartphones, Chromebooks and Cloudbooks with relatively small storage capacities of 16-64 GB. (Compared with 1TB on larger desktops and laptops). A desktop copy of Office can take up 6 GB of local hard drive storage.

- Web-based versions of major software packages are available. These include the *free* Microsoft Office Online (Word, Excel, PowerPoint, etc.,) and Google Docs, Sheets and Slides.

- These Web-based apps are slimmed down versions of the full packages but still contain all of the essential features needed for useful work.

- Web-based apps *back up* your work *automatically* to Cloud Storage, such as Google Drive, OneDrive and Dropbox. So it is *accessible on any computer* - very helpful if your usual computer is not available.

Using Web-based Apps

Whereas a *website* is mainly used to display *information*, a *Web-based app* is *interactive*, receiving input from the user, carrying out functions and sending output over the Internet to the client computer via a Web browser. Some websites include Web-based apps, such as online shopping. Anyone who uses e-mail is already using a Web-based app.

Two of the main Web-based software suites are Google Docs, Sheets and Slides, discussed below and Microsoft Office, discussed shortly. The term "Google Docs" is also used to refer to the entire Google suite including the Docs word processor, Sheets spreadsheet and Slides presentation.

Google Docs, Sheets and Slides

- These apps are available in the Google Play Store for Android devices and Chromebooks and the App Store for iOS (iPads and iPhones).

- PC machines can access Google Docs, Sheets and Slides etc., via the Google Drive and Dropbox websites, as discussed on the next page.

- Docs, Sheets and Slides are *free* and very widely used by both individuals and large organisations.

- The Google apps may not have all the elaborate features of Microsoft Office, but many of these features are not required for general work anyway.

- Documents created in Docs, Sheets and Slides are *automatically saved* in Google Drive in the Cloud and accessible on any computer with an Internet Connection.

- Google Docs, Sheets and Slides can be used to create and edit documents *offline,* where there is no Internet.

Using the Google Apps

Android, iOS and Chromebooks

The apps can be installed from the Play Store or App Store and opened on a tablet or smartphone. The option to work offline, where there is no Internet, is included in the setup.

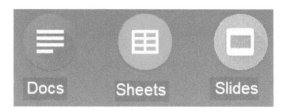

Windows PC

The Google apps can be accessed through the Google Drive and Dropbox websites in a browser such as Chrome, Firefox, Internet Explorer or Microsoft Edge, etc.

Google Drive

- Select **New** in **Drive** as shown below on the left and then select the Web-based app as shown on the right.

- **More** shown above displays further Web-based apps including Google Forms, Drawings and Pixlr Editor.

Dropbox

- Open the **dropbox.com** website and select **Files** then **Create** on the right of the screen to display the Google apps shown above and on page 149.

If you need to edit the Google files offline, this can be done using a small extra program added as an *Extension* or *Plugin* to the Google Chrome browser.

- In Chrome select the 3-dot menu, then **Settings** followed by **Extensions**.
- Make sure **Google Docs Offline** is switched On as shown in blue below on the right.

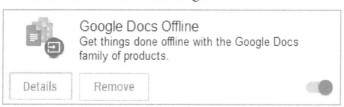

The Google web-based apps Docs, Sheets and Slides have all of the main formatting and file management features of other software such as Microsoft Word, Excel and PowerPoint, as shown by the extracts from Docs below.

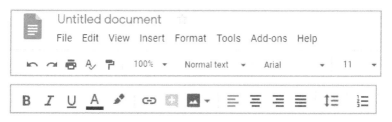

Compatibility
- Docs, Sheets and Slides can import and edit files created in the Word, Excel and PowerPoint formats. Also create files and download them in these formats.

Collaboration
- Docs, Sheets and Slides have a **Share** button enabling a link to a document to be posted in an e-mail to a friend, etc., with options to **edit**, **comment** or **view**.

Microsoft Office

This is the leading suite of software installed on desktop and laptop computers used by individuals and large organisations around the world. New, slimmed-down *online* versions of Microsoft Office have been developed for use in Cloud Computing to compete with Web-based software such as Google Docs, Sheets and Slides. The new, online versions of Word, Excel, PowerPoint and also OneNote still contain all the essential features.

- When you are online, changes made to a document, spreadsheet or presentation etc., are saved automatically to OneDrive and available on any computer on the Internet.

- When you are offline the **Autosave** feature is turned off. Changes are automatically synced up to OneDrive next time you are online.

- As discussed on page 134, a OneDrive link can be sent to allow friends or colleagues, etc., to view or edit a document, etc., in Word, Excel or PowerPoint.

Office 365

This is a subscription service, integrated with the Microsoft OneDrive Cloud Storage system. There are various payment plans, including different amounts of storage and the number of users allowed per subscription.

- You can use Word, Excel, PowerPoint, etc., *offline* but you need to go *online* every 30 days to maintain your subscription.

Windows PC

The Office 365 apps, Word, Excel, etc., can be downloaded and installed from the Microsoft Store, or during the setting up of OneDrive as discussed on pages 114–116.

Office Online

- This version of MS Office is completely free, accessed from the **Office.com** website.

- Word, Excel, PowerPoint and OneNote are opened in your Web browser, and can't be used offline.

- Office Online uses the 5 GB of Cloud Storage free with a Microsoft account.

Office Mobile

Android and iOS (iPads and iPhones)

- Free mobile apps including Word, Excel and PowerPoint are available from the Google Play Store and the Apple App Store.

- The mobile apps can be used with the free 5GB of OneDrive storage.

- Or you can to subscribe to Office 365 Personal or Home, with 1 TB or 6TB of Cloud Storage.

LibreOffice

This is another very popular, free suite of productivity software, including word processor, spreadsheet and presentation apps. LibreOffice is compatible with many file types including Word, Excel and PowerPoint.

Google Cloud Print

This app allows any computer to print documents across the Internet, via Google's Web servers, to any printer, anywhere. If you have a *Cloud Ready* printer, this should be easy to set up for Cloud Print using the manufacturer's instructions. Otherwise a *classic printer* (i.e. not Cloud Ready) will need to be set-up as follows, on a PC or Mac on a Wi-Fi network and with Google Chrome installed.

On the Windows PC or Mac Computer

* Click the Chrome icon shown right then click the 3-dot menu button and select **Settings**.

* Scroll down the screen and select **Advanced**, then **Printing**, then select **Google Cloud Print**.

* Select **Manage Cloud Print devices** and then **Classic printers**. Select **Add printers**.

* Make sure the printer attached to the PC or Mac is switched on and ticked and click **Add printer(s)**.

Printing a Document or Photo

* Open the required page or photo, etc., in Chrome.
* **PC, Mac and Chromebook:** Select **File** and **Print**.
* **Android:** Tap the 3-dot menu button, then tap **Share...** and **Print**.

* **iPad and iPhone (Using AirPrint):** Tap the **Share** button shown on the right then tap **Print**.

* **All devices:** Select the printer and print settings then finally select **Print** again to print the document.

13

Local Storage

Introduction

Despite the many advantages of Cloud computing described in the rest of this book, local storage using hard drives/SSDs and USB plug-in devices is still needed.

Some of the reasons are:

• You may be given data files on a USB device such as a flash drive or photos on an SD card removed from a DSLR camera (rather than photos taken with the camera on an Internet-ready tablet or smartphone).

• As discussed shortly, files from local storage such as an SD card or hard drive can be *uploaded* to the Cloud, so they can be accessed by any computer.

• There may be times when your Internet is not available or your router fails. *Outages* or failures of Internet services do occur, but not very often.

• Some people prefer to make *backup copies* of important files on local storage, even though Cloud Storage is normally a very secure form of backup.

• You may wish to download some files from the Cloud to the local storage such as the SSD on a tablet or smartphone. E.g. to read a book or watch a video on a flight, where the Internet is not allowed.

• Or copy some files such as photos to a USB flash drive to give to someone else, without giving them access to your entire Cloud. (Sending a *link* to a file or folder in the Cloud is discussed on page 134).

Internal Storage

This is the hard disc drive or SSD (Solid State Drive), usually labelled **OS(C:)**, built into your computer, tablet or smartphone. The SSD and the cheaper and slower *eMMC* (*embedded MultiMedia Card*) are types of flash memory with no moving parts, unlike a hard drive. Some laptops and desktops have a slot for a full size SD card, while some tablets and smartphones have a slot for a *Micro SD* card.

Desktop and Laptop Computers

- Desktop and laptop computers typically have 128GB, 256GB, 512GB or 1TB of Internal Storage. To display the **Used** and **Free space** on a Windows PC, as shown below, select the **File Explorer**, right-click over **OS(C:)** and select **Properties** from the menu.

- The desktop hard drive in the screenshot below has nearly 500GB of storage. The operating system and installed software and data files currently account for nearly 100GB, leaving nearly 400GB of free storage.

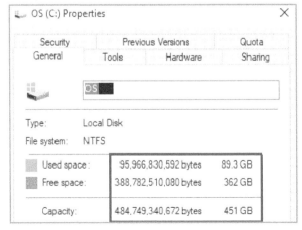

Tablets and Smartphones

Android

- Smartphones and tablets use an SSD or an eMMC as their Internal Storage instead of a hard drive, as discussed on the previous page.

- The small physical size of these mobile devices limits the Internal Storage, as shown below for a Motorola 5G Android smartphone with just 16GB.

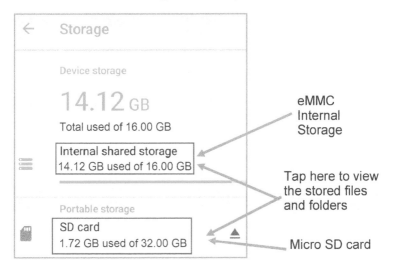

- This is displayed by tapping the **Settings** icon then selecting **Storage** from the menu.

- The 16GB Internal Storage shown above is supplemented by a 32GB Micro SD card inserted in the built-in Micro SD card slot.

- Micro SD cards up to 256GB are also available.

- Smartphones have 16GB, 32GB and 64GB Internal Storage on SSD or eMMC. This allows data to be retrieved much faster than from the Micro SD card.

- The SD card of up to 256GB mentioned on page 171 is a simple storage medium for files such as photos.

- The SSD and eMMC discussed on page 170 are more complex than the SD card. Like the rotating hard drive used on larger computers, the SSD and eMMC host the operating system and other software.

- Hence the relatively large capacity of up to 256GB available for SD cards compared with the modest 16GB to 64GB Internal Storage on tablets and smartphones.

iPad/iPhone

- Shown below is the Internal Storage on an iPad with 32GB of Internal Storage. This is displayed after selecting:

Settings > General > iPad Storage

- Other iPad models have 16GB, 64GB and 128GB of Internal Storage at various prices.

External Storage Devices

In order to supplement the limited Internal Storage on mobile devices and to transfer files between all types of computer, various external storage devices are available, as shown below.

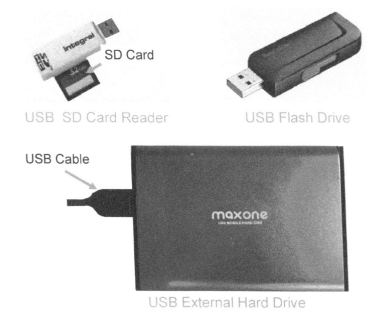

SD Card

USB SD Card Reader   USB Flash Drive

USB Cable

maxone

USB External Hard Drive

- *USB flash drives* typically have storage capacities from 8GB, 16GB, 32GB and 128GB.

- *SD cards* and *Micro SD* cards have storage capacities from 8GB to 256GB.

- *USB External hard drives* range in capacity from 120GB to 2TB.

- Some of the main units for measuring storage capacity are listed again at the top of page 174.

Units Used to Measure Storage

1 Kilobyte (KB)	=	1024 Bytes
1 Megabyte (MB)	=	1024 Kilobytes
1 Gigabyte (GB)	=	1024 Megabytes
1 Terabyte (TB)	=	1024 Gigabytes

- A *byte* is the space needed to store a letter, a digit in the range 0-9 or a keyboard character or symbol.
- Photos taken on a smartphone occupy around 1MB to 3MB. So 1GB of storage could hold approximately 300 to 1000 photos.
- On safari in Masai Mara 289 photos were taken using a DSLR camera, not a smartphone.
- The SD card from the camera was inserted into the card slot on a PC and the photos copied to the hard drive, as shown in the File Explorer extract below.

> Dropbox › Kenya

IMG_4462.JPG
JPG File
7.67 MB

IMG_4463.JPG
JPG File
7.38 MB

- The 283 photos used 2.12GB of storage and averaged approximately 7.5MB each, i.e. 133 photos per GB.
- A book similar to this one might typically take up about 10MB, when saved in the universal *PDF (Portable Document Format)* file format.
- So one tiny 2 inch 8GB flash drive could hold several hundred similar books stored as PDF files.

The removable devices shown on page 173 are all designed to plug into a standard *USB* port or socket.

Desktop and laptop computers normally have at least two USB ports built in as standard, as shown below on a Google Chromebook laptop.

USB Ports

Smartphones and tablets do not generally have full size USB ports, but an *OTG (On The Go)* cable as shown below allows them to be connected to USB devices via their battery charging port. OTG cables are available for Android devices and some iPads and iPhones. However, some iPads lack the power to operate USB connections.

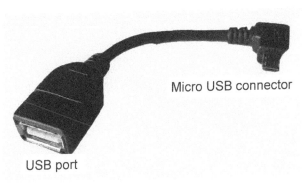

Micro USB connector

USB port

Android OTG cable

Once you've connected a USB storage device such as a flash drive, SD card/card reader or an external hard drive, it is listed in your file manager such as the Windows 10 File Explorer shown on the next page. The Chromebook file manager is known as the *Files app*.

Viewing Connected USB Devices

The USB storage devices shown on page 173 can all be connected to desktop and laptop computers, tablets and smartphones. If necessary, several USB devices can be connected simultaneously to a computer using an adapter having several USB ports. The adapter is then plugged into an OTG cable as shown on the previous page. Then they can be viewed in the relevant file manager, such as the Windows 10 File Explorer shown below.

Windows Computer

- In Windows select the File Explorer and scroll down the left-hand panel to **OS (C:)** as shown below.

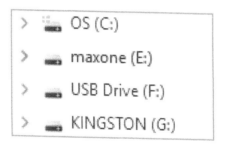

- **OS (C:)** above is the standard label for a hard drive, i.e. Internal Storage, on a Windows PC.

- **maxone (E)** is an external hard drive.

- **KINGSTON (G:)** is an 8GB flash drive.

- The **SD card** as shown in the card reader on page 173 is listed above as **USB Drive (F:)**.

- Click on the name of an external device, such as the **KINGSTON (G:)** flash drive shown above, to view the files and folders stored on it.

Android Tablet or Smartphone

- Tap the **Settings** icon then select **Storage** from the menu to open the screen shown below.

Settings

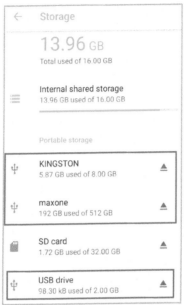

- In the above example, the plug-in USB devices are outlined in red. These are the **KINGSTON** flash drive, the **maxone** external hard drive and the **USB drive**. The latter is a full size SD card inserted in a card reader as shown on page 173.

- The **SD card** listed above is a Micro SD card inserted in the built-in Micro SD card slot in the smartphone. These are available with capacities of 16GB-256GB.

- As discussed on page 172, SD cards are simple, inexpensive storage media, offering much higher capacities than the more complex SSDs and eMMCs.

Google Chromebook

- An Acer Chromebook has two full-size USB ports to connect external devices, as shown on page 175. Tap or click the icon shown on the right to open the **Files** app and view the USB devices as shown outlined in red below.

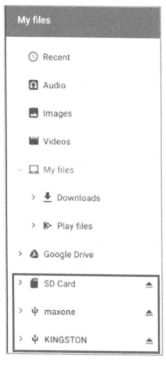

- As well as the **maxone** external hard drive and the **KINGSTON** flash drive, in the above example an **SD card** is connected to the Chromebook by a card reader, as shown on page 173.

- Tap or click any of the devices to view the stored files and folders .

Index